THE *NEW* ONE-PAGE PROJECT MANAGER

COMMUNICATE AND MANAGE ANY PROJECT WITH A SINGLE SHEET OF PAPER

CLARK A. CAMPBELL

MICK CAMPBELL

WILEY

John Wiley & Sons, Inc.

D0103662

This book is printed on acid-free paper. ∞

Cover image: Courtesy of Clark A. Campbell

Cover design: John Wiley & Sons, Inc.

Published by John Wiley & Sons, Inc., Hoboken, New Jersey.
Published simultaneously in Canada.

For general information about our other products and services, please contact our Customer Care Department within the United States at (800) 762-2974, outside the United States at (317) 572-3993 or fax (317) 572-4002.

Wiley publishes in a variety of print and electronic formats and by print-on-demand. Some material included with standard print versions of this book may not be included in e-books or in print-on-demand. If this book refers to media such as a CD or DVD that is not included in the version you purchased, you may download this material at http://booksupport.wiley.com. For more information about Wiley products, visit www.wiley.com.

Library of Congress Cataloging-in-Publication Data:

Campbell, Clark A., 1949–
  The new one-page project manager : communicate and manage any project with a single sheet of paper / Clark A. Campbell and Mick Campbell.
     p. cm.
  Rev. ed. of: The one-page project manager. c2007.
  Includes index.
  ISBN 978-1-118-37837-3 (pbk); 978-1-118-46113-6 (ebk); ISBN 978-1-118-46115-0 (ebk); ISBN 978-1-118-46147-1 (ebk)
  1. Project management. 2. Business report writing. I. Campbell, Mick, 1974- II. Campbell, Clark A., 1949- One-page project manager. III. Title.
  HD69.P75C363 2013
  658.4'04–dc23

2012032709

Printed in the United States of America

10 9 8 7 6 5 4 3

Praise for *The New One-Page Project Manager*

"The New One-Page Project Manager *is an essential part of my executive toolkit. OPPMs communicate a project's plan and then communicate progressive performance to that plan in a complete yet efficient way, thereby increasing the visibility and collaboration so vital for successful project management.*"

—Michael O. Leavitt, Chairman, Leavitt Partners; Secretary, United States Department of Health and Human Services (2005–2009); Administrator, United States Environmental Protection Agency (2003–2005); Governor of Utah (1992–2003)

"*Creating clarity from ambiguity, while organizing complex interrelated processes, lies at the heart of outstanding project management.* The New One-Page Project Manager *is a tremendous tool to assist in achieving that goal.*"

—Chris Liddell, Former CFO, Microsoft and Vice Chairman and Chief Financial Officer, General Motors

"*As the CEO of Deloitte, I had oversight of countless projects, both at Deloitte and at our clients. Successful change initiatives require clear vision, strong leadership, meaningful milestones, focused execution, and clear accountability. Clark Campbell, through* The New One-Page Project Manager, *has successfully integrated those critical success factors in one readable page. The difference between projects that succeed and those labeled as disappointments is always made in the execution. The OPPM can be an effective enabler of strong project management, significantly increasing the likelihood of success.*"

—James H. Quigley, CEO Emeritus of Deloitte

"*While at initial glance this book may appear to be simply about developing a 'dashboard' for tracking an important project, it soon becomes clear that it is much more than that. The approach outlined by Clark Campbell, an experienced and accomplished project leader, provides a proven process for project management that significantly improves the chances that the project will be completed on time, on budget, and on target for its intended purposes. Furthermore, it provides a straightforward yet compelling set of steps to ensure that those with the ability and responsibility to achieve the desired results are supported, guided, and focused in their efforts to do so. This approach will prove especially beneficial to students and practitioners who want to learn and apply the skills and tools of effective project leadership.*"

—Steven C. Wheelwright, PhD, Baker Foundation Professor,
Senior Associate Dean, Director of Publications Activities,
Harvard Business School, Harvard University

"*Impressive in its simplicity, yet universal in its application, the One-Page Project Manager began assisting Chinese project managers in 2003, when Mr. Campbell first lectured in Beijing. OPPM is easy to learn and use, and is impressive in its clear capacity to communicate. It should be required reading for every manager who wants to improve project performance, accurately tell their story, and do it efficiently.*"

—Jonathan H. Du, PhD, CEO and Chairman,
WiseChina Training Ltd., Beijing, China

"*Total Lean Management requires lean communication. OPPM is in very deed—a lean communication tool. O.C. Tanner, a Shingo Prize winner, is among the top 3 percent of Lean companies in North America. Their distinctive combination of OPPM with Toyota's A3 report reveals a unique, continuous improvement, one that documents, in part, how they have executed their strategy to achieve market dominance and profitable growth.*"

—Ross E. Robson, PhD, President DNR Lean LLC,
Strategic Founder and Executive Director of the Shingo Prize (retired)

"*Don't be fooled into thinking that OPPM is applicable only to monumental and product related tasks. OPPM is a way of organizing the way one thinks about tasks that lie ahead. It is a way to identify what goals are worth the investment of time and other resources, and then to describe them in simple and measurable terms. It is just as useful in building a winning little league team as it is in building a ball field. Once understood, OPPM is a tool useful for any task important enough to plan for.*"

—Justice Michael J. Wilkins, Utah Supreme Court (retired)

To Tracy

CONTENTS

You have in your hands a book that is both a critical tool for, and a symbol of, our innovation economy.

Our twenty-first-century workplace is the scene of rapid, visible evolution. This rapid evolution means we are surrounded by projects. Some projects are huge, such as a new commercial airplane model. But the proliferation of projects is due more to an increase in small projects, such as implementing standardized processes in an operating room, a promotion campaign for a winery, or opening a new office for a growing business. There are many reasons the pace of change and the number of projects are increasing, but there is no doubt it is true, for the evidence is all around us.

Projects generate chaos. How could they not? The definition of a project is *work that has a beginning and an end, and produces a unique product or service.* By their nature, every project has an element of discovery, doing something that hasn't been done exactly that way before. Every project is different from the last one. It's the opposite of the twentieth-century focus on continuous process improvement — refining the way we manufacture a car or process a bank loan until we drive out all inefficiency and error. Managing a single project may not quite constitute chaos, but as projects proliferate we find ourselves juggling a collection of increasingly diverse tasks, goals, and resources.

The project-driven workplace emerged in the 1990s. In that one decade, the discipline of project management broke out of its construction and defense industry niche and spread throughout all organizations: for-profit, nonprofit, and government. With it came an explosion of training, methodology, software, and certification—all directed toward gaining control over the ever-increasing complexity associated with managing more and more projects.

Our approach to managing the complexity of projects has become equally complex. Project Management Offices (PMOs) are staffed with expert project managers. Enterprise project management software attempts to systematize the juggling game, corralling our jumble of projects into a common framework and database. All of this effort and structure introduced to get our arms around this chaotic work has allowed us to juggle more and bigger projects.

Yet there have been two significant departures from this trend toward larger, more complex project management. The first, the Agile software development approach, broke the paradigm of rigidity and control because it became clear that increased structure both slowed projects down and degraded the quality and usefulness of the resulting software. Within a decade, the appeal of Agile transcended the software and information technology industries and is being used with other kinds of projects where discovery and rapid learning play major roles in project success. Agile does acknowledge the complexity of projects, but it addresses the complexity with principles and techniques that are designed to coexist with complexity rather than conquer it.

The second significant trend away from complex project management is described in this book, *The One-Page Project Manager*, or OPPM. The OPPM also accepts that projects can be large and complex, but insists that to effectively manage them we must be able to distill the complexity to bring the major themes into focus. Using the OPPM, we can simultaneously pay attention to several key dimensions of project performance, producing a sufficiently complete understanding to make good decisions.

How is it possible that we can manage a major project using the information formatted onto a single page? Even simple project management methodologies call for a half dozen separate documents. But that is the magic and the value of the OPPM. Project management is already a discipline populated by graphic techniques, because a picture not only is worth a thousand words, but it may be the only way to truly synthesize and digest the meaning of those words. The OPPM takes synthesis and summary to a new level.

During 20-plus years of teaching and consulting in the field of project management, my team at The Versatile Company has worked with many thousands of projects and project managers in industries as diverse as health care, education, aerospace, and government. Throughout this time I have prized the practical over the theoretical. I particularly attempt to focus on the minimum management overhead that produces the greatest productivity benefit, so it is natural for me to appreciate the OPPM. I am also naturally skeptical, so I was cautious in embracing it. I've developed my own rules of thumb for evaluating a project and the minimums needed for effective management, and they are published as the Five Project Success Factors in my own popular book, *The Fast Forward MBA in Project Management*, 4th edition (John Wiley & Sons, 2012). I used the lens of the five factors to view the OPPM and was impressed that it contributed to every one of them.

1. *Agreement among the project team, customers, and management on the goals of the project.* The OPPM clearly and concisely states the project's goal at the top of the page, with subobjectives listed in the left column. Together, these provide clarity to key stakeholders about the purpose and scope of the project.

2. *A plan that shows an overall path and clear respon-sibilities and that can be used to measure progress during the project.* This may be the OPPM's greatest strength—synthesizing and summarizing the details of the project plan and task status to provide a useful high-level understanding of the plan and our progress.

3. *A controlled scope.* Uncontrolled scope is the num-ber one threat to on-time, on-budget performance. Uncontrolled scope means we allow additional tasks and objectives to be added to a project without con-sciously and formally accepting the related cost and

schedule increases. Using the OPPM, it is clear what our major tasks are, when we will meet major schedule milestones, and how much we plan to spend. Changes that attempt to creep into the project will become visible in one or more of these dimensions quickly, providing notification to the project manager and the project's owners that they need to contain the change.

4. *Management support.* Every project needs support from management. Project managers and teams don't have sufficient authority to accomplish the project on their own. The age-old problem is getting busy executives to engage based on accurate project information. This was the genesis of the OPPM: creating a single project dashboard that enables meaningful, informed involvement from managers with multiple projects under their span of control.

5. *Constant, effective communication among everyone involved in the project.* This is the essence of the OPPM.

Amazingly, the OPPM is the product of a very few executives—and of one in particular, Clark Campbell. Among all the other methods and techniques in the world of project management, it is nearly impossible to find one with a single inventor, as most techniques have evolved out of common usage across hundreds or thousands of projects. The clear exception is Henry Gantt, who literally a century ago introduced the now ubiquitous chart that bears his name. Like Gantt, Clark

Campbell and his colleagues produced this new graphic for project reporting out of necessity and honed its design through use.

This new edition benefits from five years of feedback since its initial publication in 2007. Appropriately, it also includes a modified OPPM for Agile.

In our innovation economy characterized by rapid evolution and abundant projects, project management has taken on increased importance. It is also necessary to realize that we need both complex and simple approaches to managing projects. The OPPM does not replace the complex methods—Clark Campbell is clear about that. The OPPM creates an interface between the sophisticated, specialized skills of professional project managers and the many other project stakeholders whose expertise is needed for the project.

I congratulate Clark on his success pioneering this timely management and communication tool. It is well suited to the demands of leadership in these turbulent times.

Eric Verzuh, PMP
President, The Versatile Company,
www.VersatileCompany.com
Author, *The Fast Forward MBA
in Project Management*, 4th edition

ACKNOWLEDGMENTS

In addition to those foundational contributors acknowledged in the first three OPPM books, we are profoundly grateful for the insight, contributions, and support from:

Alan Horowitz—our friend, writer, and critical thinker.

Lauren Elkins—agile consultant and Master Scrum Master.

Governor Michael O. Leavitt—visionary and OPPM innovator.

Jared Stout and Steve Whipple—International contributors.

Byron Terry—Microsoft Excel guru.

Eric Sokol and George Mentz—marketers and certifiers.

Shannon Vargo, Deborah Schindlar, Elana Schulman, and the team at John Wiley & Sons.

Tracy, Annie, Emma, Abe, Jane, Kate, Chris, and Karen for confidence in and inspiration for Mick.

Meredith, Marjorie, and family for patience with and encouragement for Clark.

Finally, gratitude is extended to a continually expanding group of companies and individual OPPM users for collaboration, skilled deployments, and best practices in communicating project plans, and communicating performance to those plans.

Seventeen years ago, a skeleton of the *One-Page Project Manager* (OPPM) was crafted in the Cincinnati airport by a small project team while we waited for a delayed flight. Our company president had asked us to find a way to collect the necessary project components, wrap them around a standard X-chart, and report to him on a single page.

That sounded nearly impossible. Project reports for upper management typically ran to many, often dozens, of pages, so we were certainly in favor of exploring ways to eliminate any non-value-added work. We therefore crafted the first OPPM to document the plan and communicate the progress for a project to design and build a $10 million warehouse with automated storage and distribution. Then, for the next decade, we used the OPPM to communicate the status of projects of all sizes and also to actually manage small projects.

It has now been seven years since work was started on my book *The One-Page Project Manager*, where the OPPM templates and methods were shared with project managers and other interested practitioners. Since that initial publication, I have taught project management at the University of Utah and Westminster College in Salt Lake City and have consulted with Fortune 500 companies and taught seminars in the United States and abroad. Two additional books followed, *The One-Page Project Manager for IT Projects* and *The One-Page Project Manager for Execution*, written with O.C. Tanner and Westminster colleague Mike Collins.

Another considerable change is that after 30 years I retired from the O.C. Tanner Company and founded OPPM International (OPPMi) with my son Michael (Mick) Campbell. At OPPMi, we provide web-based project management tools and write, consult, train, and speak around the world on both traditional and agile methods, as well as on how to use the OPPM. Interacting with thousands of folks has considerably enhanced our understanding of the communication issues project managers face every day and how the OPPM has become part of the solution.

Finally, readers of all the OPPM books—and more than 100,000 copies have been sold in seven languages—have been gracious and generous in their feedback. They have told us numerous stories about their use of the OPPM, its benefits, and the challenges encountered when incorporating this tool into their project management processes. From their comments we have learned an enormous amount, and thank them for their observations.

Comments from Readers and Users*

OPPM provided me with valuable benefits which will make me and my company more productive. The lessons and insights gleaned from Mick and Clark were very interesting as well as valuable. I highly recommend!
—E. McCasland, Dell Telephone Cooperative

---

*Mick has collected these comments from readers and users who have read our books, have attended his seminars, and have used the OPPM.

Combining this feedback and experience, we decided not to call this a second edition but to retitle the book, *The New One-Page Project Manager.*

It is new in two ways: updated and expanded. It is an *update* of the first book with some content from the second and third, and it is *expanded*, both in quantity and scope. Quantitatively, this book contains additional templates and displays. In terms of scope, it includes a discussion of the agile OPPM, references to the Project Management Body of Knowledge (PMBOK), coverage of the OPPM as a marketing tool, illustrations of how the OPPM aligns to current communication research, and all of this—finally—with templates in *color!*

70 YEARS OF EXPERIENCE

In January 1962, when I was a 12-year-old in junior high school, Dad passed away in his sleep. Mother, a government secretary, then tackled the challenge of raising my younger brother, my two younger sisters, and me.

To keep me engaged and out of trouble, mother assigned me a "project" to build in our unfinished basement. I, of course, knew very little about carpentry, electricity, heating, or any project management methods.

Fortunately, we lived in a neighborhood with plenty of SMEs—subject matter experts—although we didn't call them that at the time. One neighbor owned a building supply company, another was an electrician, and another did heating and air-conditioning. I arranged for them to provide some needed help but had to do most of the work myself. As a young teenager, unbeknownst to me, I had been given a most valuable gift. From that early formative experience, I learned many of the basics of project management, one failure at a time. A passion for project management was born.

As I write this, I am 63. That's a half-century where nearly every professional responsibility and assignment that came my way required project management in one form or another.

As a student publisher of the campus newspaper and then president of the student body, projects were what captured my interest. Two years in London saw me gravitate to revising and publishing reports on volunteer service. Tasks as an economic analyst for the government were project based. My first real job was as a young MBA/chemical engineer with DuPont assigned to the Kevlar commercialization project. DuPont was deeply committed to communicating via graphs and charts and tutored me in the visual display of data. In 1979 I joined O.C. Tanner to manage a dozen internal consulting projects. I continued to direct projects for the next three decades, retiring as chief project officer and senior vice president.

Mick, as I said, is my partner at OPPM International, which we started in 2008. Agile methods, information technology (IT), and computer projects were the focus of his master's degree and eventual position as vice president for a mid-sized telecom company. He brings 20 years (he is now 38) of experience to our work, including both traditional and agile project management. His Cisco certifications and insights into lean and agile project management, coupled with his understanding of the PMBOK, have refined and enlarged the content, tools, and techniques introduced in this book.

Comments from Readers and Users

Phenomenal learning environment. What a pleasure to have both Mick and Clark Campbell available to present the material. I was honored to have the opportunity to hear "The One-Page Project Manager" presented by this father–son team. It doesn't get any better than that. The wealth of experience and working knowledge Mick and Clark possess is absolutely invaluable.

—J. Fenton-Sims, Allstate

PROJECT MANAGEMENT: A BRIEF HISTORY

The Microsoft Office website notes that in the latter half of the nineteenth century, large-scale government projects became the basis for project management methodology. Modern project management dates from the 1950s and 1960s.

During the early years of project management's modern history, timelines and PERT (program evaluation and review technique) scheduling techniques were the most commonly taught methods. Construction, engineering, defense, and aerospace were the drivers of more formal methods, with Primavera (now owned by Oracle) launching its project management tools in 1983.

IT projects themselves began to be aggressively supported with the launch of Microsoft Project in 1990.

Agile project management is of more recent vintage. According to John C. Goodpasture in his book *Project Management the Agile Way*, this form of project management began in Japan in the 1980s for use in the product development industry. It was in response to new products often not meeting expectations. Agile project management got on a more formal footing in 2001, when a group of project management thinkers gathered in Snowbird, Utah, to find common ground among competing and untraditional methods and produced a framework it named the Agile Manifesto. From this came the Agile Principles and the Agile Alliance.

Today, project management is an academic discipline, a business activity, and a strategy—indeed, a profession. A growing demand for project management tools has fueled the development of a broad array of software, methodologies, and applications, each seeking to aid project managers in their pursuit for project success. There exist publications and websites that cover only issues related to project management. A small library could be compiled consisting exclusively of books about project management. Training organizations, seminars, and certifications focus exclusively on the topic. A Google search today reveals more than 200 million results. Dozens of universities offer master's degrees in the discipline, and a few offer doctorates. A topic and a skill set that were originally developed on an ad hoc basis are today a significant industry, profession, and topic of academic study.

The Necessity of Simplicity and the Power of Visuals

Not a single project manager would disagree with the necessity of simplicity or that a "picture is worth a thousand words."

The difficulty arises in our attempts to find that elusive balance between too little and too much and in crafting just the right visual.

For us project managers, the "detail syndrome" seriously compromises this quest. Yes, the detail syndrome—you have it, and so do I. We have been successful project managers in large measure because we understand and focus on the details, we manage and drive the details, we constantly think about the details, we know which details are critical to our project's success, and we want management to appreciate the complexity of our efforts.

However, our attempts to communicate often include too much detail.

Now before moving on, let me make it clear that this propensity for both detail awareness and management is indeed essential to successful project management, yet it can add confusion to, and dilute the clarity of, our project communication.

Okay, still no debate. Yes, we should communicate simply even when it feels counterintuitive. So how do we know how much is too much? Mick calls this the quest for "serious simplicity."

Edward R. Tufte is professor emeritus at Yale University, where he taught courses in statistical evidence and information design. In his remarkable book *The Visual Display of Quantitative Information,* 2nd ed. (Cheshire, CT: Graphics Press, 2001), he says, "Often the most effective way to describe, explore, and summarize a set of numbers—even a very large set—is to look at pictures of those numbers. Furthermore, of all methods for analyzing and communicating statistical information, well-designed data graphics are usually the simplest and at the same time the most powerful."

Einstein is reputed to have said, "Everything should be made as simple as possible, but no simpler."

THE GUIDING PRINCIPLE

Be as simple as is practicable.

Practicable is precisely the right word here. Serious simplicity is not just as simple as possible, but as simple as practicable. *Practicable* has roots in Medieval Latin (*practicabilis*, meaning "capable of being used") and Greek (*praktikos*, meaning "fit for action"). Synonyms would include *achievable, attainable, feasible*, and *executable*.

I have had the privilege to travel and speak together with other authors in the "Nationally Renowned Best Selling Authors in the Project Management" series sponsored by the Project Management Resource Group. One member of our group, Michael J. Cunningham, president and founder of the Harvard Computing Group, writes in his book *Finish What You Start: 10 Surefire Ways to Deliver Your Projects On Time and On Budget* (New York: Kaplan Publishing, 2006), "One of the most complex issues about larger-scale project management is *visualizing* what is happening. *Communication* may be time consuming and might not appear to produce immediate results, but trust me, *this is the big one*" (italics added).

A wristwatch provides a useful visual and metaphor for project management. The elegant transparent face of Swiss-made Vacheron Constantin watches in Figure 1.1 show both the time and a visual display of the movements, all working in perfect harmony to determine, convey, and then maintain the correct time.

FIGURE 1.1   *Visual Movement Watches*

FIGURE 1.2   *Simple Watch Face*

A project manager, like the watch-maker, knows every cog, spring, post, jewel, and movement. The principle purpose of a watch, however, is not to reveal its workings, but to simply communicate the time. See Figure 1.2.

Project managers are prone to communicate project status with pages of paragraphs and comprehensive visuals—not dissimilar, metaphorically, to communicating the time with watches like those in Figure 1.1. This is because of the following:

1. We are inflicted with detail syndrome. "We are the watchmakers."

2. We sense that by exposing more of the project's "inner workings" our conclusions will be more credible. "You can see why this watch keeps perfect time."

3. We are fully conversant with all the details and quite at home with their interrelationships. "I find satisfaction in working with, and in observing the inner workings of, my watches."

4. We want others to know *what* we know and also to know *that* we know. "See how complicated this watch is, and I was the one who built it."

5. We allow a request for one detail to open a floodgate for revealing many details. "Because you asked for the date, I'm sure you will appreciate the day, the month, the phases of the moon, and more."

6. We already know the status and therefore are not able to perceive the distraction magnified by a veil of details. "It is clear to me what time it is."

7. Finally, some of our bosses want all the details. Selected discerning customers are certainly willing and able to invest in the stunning timepieces shown in Figure 1.1.

Jeffrey Kluger, senior writer at *TIME* magazine, muses in his best-selling book *Simplexity: Why Simple Things Become Complex* (New York: Hyperion, 2009), "Complexity, as any scientist will tell you, is a slippery idea. Things that seem complicated can be preposterously simple; things that seem simple can be dizzyingly complex. We're suckers for scale."

Comments from Readers and Users

OPPM's approach to simplification of reporting and status is a great value. Status reports rebuild the whole watch rather than simply showing where we are and what is needed next.

—C. Burnside, FEMA

The one-page project manager (OPPM) obliges project managers to communicate in a sufficient, and yet efficient, way. It compels them to communicate just the right balance of too much and too little. Using our watch metaphor, the OPPM is the watch face and not the watch mechanics. Stakeholders are not generally interested in a project's mechanics (details deep into the work-breakdown-structure or financial minutia or comprehensive task dependencies), but just the essential pieces of information on how the project is progressing on schedule, task, cost, quality, and risk deliverables.

It has been fascinating to observe how the OPPM is an effective communication tool. We have watched as those who knew virtually nothing about it found it could be read without much training, almost as readily as a watch by a child who has recently learned to tell time. As in Figure 1.2, watches are designed to simply communicate the time. The OPPM is designed to communicate project status simply and intuitively.

Over the years, Mick and I have conducted OPPM training sessions in Europe, Asia, Canada, the Caribbean, and many major American cities, at which we have handed out sample OPPMs to thousands of attendees before they receive any training with it. Consistently, they have understood much of it after a few minutes of study. And with no more than 15 minutes of clarification to explain aspects of the tool that are not immediately apparent, these project managers can read and understand the entire OPPM. If you want an example of simplicity in communication, I think I can say, without hubris, look at the OPPM.

Comments from Readers and Users

I've heard about OPPM, but didn't think it could help me. After seeing how it is created, I know it to be an extremely useful tool to track projects and communicate status.
—D. Harrington, ELCAN Optical Technologies

The 1848 Shaker song by Elder Joseph Brackett begins, "'Tis a gift to be simple, 'tis a gift to be free, 'tis a gift to come down where we ought to be." OPPM has proved to be a simple gift to those wrestling with project management communication.

Remembering Einstein, it would be a gift only if it were not *too* simple. The power and simplicity of OPPM is a combination of the following:

1. All five essential parts of a project (tasks, objectives, timeline, cost, and owners) plus risk and quality
2. The linkages and alignment of each
3. A clear, efficient, and accurate representation of both plan and performance
4. An addition to, rather than a replacement of, current powerful project management tools
5. An intuitive picture that is easy to create and easy to maintain

Comments from Readers and Users

Most valuable—learning the OPPM methodology. I have been searching for simplicity and easy communication skills. Hearing the message to focus more on communication and be simple was valuable.

—K. Gray, Enterasys

THE POWER OF VISUALS

The power of the OPPM comes from its use of graphics. This is not a new idea. Those old enough to remember the early days of the personal computer in the 1980s and early 1990s remember what it was like to operate those machines. Most used an operating system known as DOS (which had versions from IBM and Microsoft) and required the user to type in instructions in cryptic codes. For example, backup c:\oppm*.* d: /s tells the computer to back up all the files and subdirectories in the OPPM directory found on the c: drive and save them to the d: drive.

Professor Margaret J. Wheatley, in her book *Leadership and the New Science: Discovering Order in a Chaotic World*, 3rd ed. (San Francisco: Berrett-Koehler, 2006), concludes, "Our yearning for simplicity is one we share with natural systems."

Today computers use graphical user interfaces, commonly called GUIs, which allow the user to save files by clicking with a mouse or tapping with one's finger on the "save" icon (a graphic) and directing it to save wherever on the device the user wants. In Apple's iTunes, for example, to take a song in your music library and save it to another place, such as a playlist, just click on the song and drag and drop it into the desired playlist—no typing, no text. It's all about the graphical depiction of drag and drop.

The reason the OPPM communicates with simplicity and clarity is because it, like today's computers, relies on displays, graphics, and images. These visual depictions in general have remarkable power to convey a great deal of information, quickly, accurately, and with clarity. Before children learn to speak and long before they learn to read, they often can recognize visuals like drawings and photos. Understanding visual representations seems an innate ability.

No one would think of describing the outline and features of a country or region with words alone; maps are infinitely more effective and clear. When traveling and wanting to convey one's experiences and adventures to friends and family, most people rely far more on photographs and videos than words. Television, YouTube, and movies attract billions of viewers precisely because they are visual media.

By using graphics, the OPPM is able to provide the reader with a project's essence, its essentials, not its underlying nuts and bolts or cogs and wheels.

Yale professor Edward Tufte, in helping us understand how something can be explained, teaches what he calls the Five Grand Principles of Analytical Design.

1. Show comparisons.
2. Show causality.
3. Show multivariate data.
4. Show "whatever it takes."
5. Show documentation.

The OPPM is assembled to display each of these five principles.

CRITICAL PATH METHOD AND EARNED VALUE MANAGEMENT

Well established in the project management profession are two elegantly simple metrics designed to convey information and meaning simply and with clarity. First is the critical path method, or CPM, which came out of DuPont in the 1950s. Its objective is to calculate and communicate the shortest completion time possible for a project and highlight those critical tasks, which, if delayed, would delay the whole project.

By design, the OPPM's tasks do not show dependencies; therefore, a critical path is not readily apparent. Experience has shown that full PERT (program evaluation and review technique) charts and graphical network illustrations of the work breakdown structure, although essential to hands-on project managers for large projects, often tend to overcommunicate and therefore don't communicate well to important stakeholders. The typical CPM Gantt chart visual is not part of the OPPM. When CPM is important,

OPPM users identify these tasks by showing their task numbers in red. In this way, critical path tasks are communicated to stakeholders simply.

The second is earned value management, or EVM, which emerged in the 1960s, when the US Department of Defense established a computation and communication approach using a set of 35 criteria. Industry has now codified EVM in the ANSI EIA 748-A standard. Calculations can be complex, but the intent is to appraise and drive improvement in project scope, schedule, and cost with the simple comparison of earned value to planned and actual performance. The driving idea is to show project performance with two numbers—the schedule performance index (SPI) and the cost performance index (CPI).

For most, the two earned value indices by themselves are insufficient and often expensive, especially when considering the cost of maintaining the requisite data.

The basic OPPM shows a bar in the lower-right section representing planned project cost. Actual cost is shown on a comparative bar with both an amount and a color indicating the seriousness of any overruns. Without the performance-to-schedule shown above in the middle of the OPPM, the cost comparison graph is insufficient because with that data alone, you don't know whether you are getting the value (scope and timing) you wanted for what you planned to pay.

EVM is specifically designed to address these issues by simply comparing value earned with value planned, which is information found in the OPPM. Where required, EVM can be shown in the cost metric section of your OPPM with color and numerical designations.

NOW TO TURN THINGS 180 DEGREES — BEWARE OF BEING TOO SIMPLE

Simpler is not always better. Because complexity is well recognized as a culprit of poor communication, it is not surprising that those in project management have attempted to instill too much simplicity—sometimes to the detriment of what they are communicating.

Do not equate simplicity with brevity. You can be very brief and communicate poorly. A concise description of over or under budget alone is not enough, however. What appears to be under budget—good news—could really be bad news with reduced spending resulting primarily from delayed work. Also, apparent over budget bad news could really be good news because extra expenditures have produced greater scope in less time than originally planned.

Consider this quote from US Supreme Court Justice Oliver Wendell Holmes, Jr.: "I wouldn't give a fig for the simplicity on this side of complexity; I would give my life for the simplicity on the far side of complexity." In the phrase "I wouldn't give a fig for the simplicity on this side of complexity," Holmes is saying he is uninterested in getting a shorthand version of something that does not convey all that is important, say like someone who reads the Cliff Notes for a novel instead of the novel itself. But the phrase "I would give my life for the simplicity on the far side of complexity" is saying he seriously values communications that simply and adequately convey, elicited by full understanding, the essence of a subject.

An example of a succinct project status report occurred between novelist Victor Hugo and the publisher of his masterwork, *Les Misérables*. Wondering whether the publisher's work on his book was complete, Hugo sent a telegram whose message was in its entirety: "?" The publisher replied with a message of equal brevity: "!" Hugo wanted to know the status of his book, and the publisher understood it from the question mark, and Hugo understood that the book was complete from the publisher's exclamation mark.

I like to think the OPPM can, simply and adequately, convey the essence of a project. And by using it, you can be on the side Holmes so greatly valued.

Comments from Readers and Users

OPPM—this will revolutionize how my team and I present information. Simple, yet powerful!
—F. Griffin, Northrop Grumman

OPPM Is All about Communication

Imagine it is Friday afternoon and your company's president just told you he must report to the board of directors about your project and its status during their lunch break on Monday. He asks for a summary of your project that uses text, graphs, and charts—including what aspects of it are on, ahead, or behind schedule; who is responsible for each of the project's major tasks; how the project is performing in terms of the budget; how well the project is meeting its objectives; what major problems have cropped up; generally how well the project is presently progressing; and a forecast for the next three months.

Providing all this information could fill a book. You consider calling up Microsoft Project, Oracle's Primavera, or another project management software program you have been diligently using and compiling all the data he requested.

One thing holding you back is the time required to prepare such a report. You and your team are deploying a major milestone this weekend, and a report like this will take up a lot of energy that would otherwise go to the project. The performance of the project could suffer because your president wants such a comprehensive report in such a short time.

In addition, you know the board will, at best, be very limited on time. Senior managers usually only have the time to read the highlights. They cannot read an entire multipage report; instead, they look for key indicators and the most vital information. If your report proves incomplete or unsatisfactory, they will be relentless in pursuit of understanding. Therefore, you must be thorough and disclose both good and bad news.

What do you do? Should you delay your deployment and devote the weekend and some of your best people to preparing such a report, or should you do the best you can, alone, and hope the board is diverted by other issues prior to their lunch and therefore not as piercing as usual?

The best solution is actually neither of these. What you should do—and what you should have done from the beginning of your project—is simply provide a copy of your one-page project manager (OPPM). It can be done quickly, easily, and without endangering the project's performance. All the information required is summarized on one page using intuitive graphics that even the busiest senior manager and board member will quickly comprehend.

Comments from Readers and Users

Most valuable was the OPPM. It provides exactly what I would like to share with my stakeholders with the correct amount of detail.
—B. Ingram, JPMorgan Chase

That is the promise of the OPPM: to convey all salient information a project's stakeholders need to know in a timely, easy-to-understand, and easy-to-compile format. From my experience in managing dozens of projects—ranging from celebrating the bicentennial of the US Constitution with Chief Justice Warren Burger, to implementing an SAP enterprise-wide solution, to building an award distribution center, to winning a coveted management prize, to reengineering a major business process, to launching a new Internet business, to gaining ISO 9000 certification—the OPPM works. And readers of my books confirm that my experience with the OPPM is not unusual because they have effectively used the tool for untold numbers of their own projects.

The OPPM informs, keeps people focused on what is important, makes clear who is responsible for what, and tracks how well the project is performing based on several variables—all on one, simple 8½-inch-by-11-inch piece of paper. OPPM neatly balances management's need to know with its desire to know just enough in an easy-to-read format. It answers more questions than it generates, which is why it is such an effective communications tool.

Remember the adage "A picture is worth a thousand words." The *Wall Street Journal* reported on an academic study that found "humans process information 17 times faster using sight than other senses."

The OPPM takes advantage of our ability to grasp lots of data and concepts when presented in visual form. The idea that people often understand pictures better than words is not new. What is new is the use of visuals to provide detailed, essential information in the project management world.

 No matter what the project — its goals or its purpose, large or small — certain aspects of managing a project are consistent. And one of these consistencies is the need to communicate.

Communication Is Key

Certainly, much has been written about communicating among the team members of a project. The 1,100-plus-page textbook on project management *Project Management,* 10th ed. (Hoboken, NJ: John Wiley & Sons, 2009), by Harold Kerzner notes: "Because of the time spent in a communications mode, the project manager may very well have as his or her responsibility the process of *communications management*" (italics added).

Communications management is the formal or informal process of conducting or supervising the exchange of information upward, downward, laterally, or diagonally. In short, the main business of project managers may be communication. There appears to be a direct correlation between the project manager's ability to manage the communications process and project performance.

This book is about project management communication and therefore project performance. It is about straight talk that adequately and efficiently illustrates the whole story. But unlike anything I've ever seen written about project management communications, this book is primarily about communicating with those who are not part of the project, both inside and outside the organization. Yes, every project has an audience who, although not directly involved in it, is deeply interested in the project, yet few project managers know how to effectively communicate with this constituency.

This constituency includes the board of directors, senior management, suppliers, customers, and superiors or subordinates, among others, who are indirectly involved with the project or its outcome. Project managers who poorly communicate with these constituencies may find themselves in difficult situations no matter how well a project is progressing.

Comments from Readers and Users

For me, the most valuable tool is "The One-Page Project Manager." We have been struggling to find a format for status reporting that will both satisfy the business owners and the working team. This tool will be perfect—clearly laying out graphically the status of the project for the business owners, and the tasks and risks for the working team.

—M. Li, JetBlue

 **CONCEPT** Your success as a project manager is in direct proportion to your ability to communicate project performance (that is, scope, timeliness, and planned versus actual resources), current completions, and future expectations.

Management wants to know about projects, particularly larger ones. Even small projects have managers at some level in the corporate hierarchy who have an interest or responsibility for the project yet are not directly part of the project. Bigger projects tend to attract the attention of more and more upper-level managers, with the biggest projects getting on the radar screen of the chief executive officer (CEO) and even the board of directors.

Comments from Readers and Users

I think the OPPM should be a must for any organization and all project managers. It will help any project manager and project team understand the deliverables and always exceed expectations. As you utilize and follow OPPM it will bring consistency to your projects.

—W. Loban, Fluor

Obert C. Tanner, the founder of the company where I worked, was intimately involved with our building projects, no matter how small or large. These were of great interest to him. However, he left computer software projects, even very large ones, to others from whom he expected simple reports of these complex projects' parameters.

These not-directly-involved managers, like Tanner, don't want to spend a great deal of time studying the status of a project. If a supervisor on the project team isn't performing, management wants to know this but doesn't want to spend time and effort ferreting out the why and who. Whether a part of a project is running behind or is on time, or if a part is over budget, under budget, or on budget—these are things management wants to know. Management wants to know what's going on, who is performing well, who needs help, and what the overall status is of the project.

But—and this is important—they want to know this easily and quickly. Those not directly involved with a project but who have a vested interest in seeing it successfully completed need to be communicated with in a way that engages them and doesn't waste their time. Long reports, detailed analyses of a project, and extended discussions of what's going on—well, these are almost certain to cause a manager's immediate attention to divert to other pressing issues.

KEY CONCEPT When asked to write a project status report, many project managers produce shallow or incomplete summaries in an attempt to make them short. Many such reports prompt more questions than they answer. In such cases, brevity breeds confusion. The OPPM answers more questions than it generates and is brief but sufficient, which is why it is such an effective communication tool.

Yet, when you read all that's written about project management, including all the articles and textbooks with hundreds and hundreds of pages, you'll find very little about how to communicate succinctly and effectively with supervisors who have an interest in a project but are not directly involved. There is a lot written about what Kerzner called communications management, but such discussions almost invariably involve how to communicate among members of the project team. Little is written about communicating to corporate management and even less about how to communicate in a way that accommodates management's need for efficiency and ease of understanding.

Comments from Readers and Users

I believe the OPPM ideology and report has the potential to be a powerful tool in my organization. There are so many reports that we deliver so often and the bottom line is difficult to extrapolate from them. The OPPM provides the bottom line front and center.
—S. Ramirez, California State University San Marcos

Since writing the first OPPM book, I have spoken in various cities along with Andy Crowe. Crowe's book *Alpha Project Management: What the Top 2% Know That*

Everyone Else Does Not (Kennesaw, GA: Velociteach, 2006), concludes that, "Of all the attributes that separate the Alpha group from their peers, communication presents the most striking difference." He goes on to say, "Few topics evoked the emotional response that communications did. . . . This was their single greatest need."

His research revealed that project managers lack two key communications skills:

1. Understanding of their audience's communications needs
2. An awareness of how their communication was received

Crowe then described the top four traits that distinguished the top 2 percent:

1. The alphas talk to stakeholders very early in the project.
2. The alphas set a communication schedule.
3. The alphas communicate their message in a complete, clear, and concise manner.
4. The alphas create an open channel, regularly talking with stakeholders about the communication itself.

From this, Mick and I have boiled down Crowe's insights into four short prescriptions, which we call the Alpha Four:

1. Collaborate early.
2. Establish a cadence.

3. Craft clear, concise, and complete messages.

4. Open a channel for continuous improvement.

The OPPM aligns nicely with the Alpha Four and is a tool that was designed, from the beginning, as a way to engage upper management and all stakeholders and make their jobs easier.

What Is the One-Page Project Manager?

I go into detail later about the makeup of the one-page project manager (OPPM) and how to build one, but for now I offer a simple OPPM definition: **the OPPM is a communication tool for informing project stakeholders.**

The OPPM paints a highly visual, interlocking picture of a project. It displays, relates, and links various project components, making immediately clear to stakeholders the plan and then the performance to that plan. Because names of responsible people are shown, motivation is magnified and opportunities for appreciation are amplified. A simple open circle, or bubble, indicates work planned during its corresponding time box. When the planned work is complete, the bubble is filled in. Comparing open and filled bubbles to the current date reveals timely performance of the scheduled tasks. Stoplight colors (red, yellow, and green) also highlight project performance and risk mitigation.

Driving the development of the OPPM was the acknowledgment that we at O.C. Tanner lacked, as a management team, the discipline to consistently manage projects to achieve on-time and on-budget results. We just didn't have the skills needed to successfully manage projects on a consistent basis. The solution, we thought, was to send our managers to project management school, which we did. We also read many books and hired plenty of consultants—and got mired in project management theory and details.

The minutia of projects—exhaustive planning, the filling out of forms (we had 25 different forms), and so on—became our focus, and we got overwhelmed by the bureaucracy, which seriously affected our execution. This well-intentioned drive toward improved project management died of its own weight. We realized we were concentrating more on the process and paperwork and therefore less on project performance.

The first OPPM (see Figure 3.1) came about as a coagulation of ideas relating to organizing parts of a project around a simple matrix suggested by our then president, Kent Murdock. Being a trial lawyer in a former life, Murdock was used to simplifying complex issues into summaries sufficient to address the salient facts yet efficiently persuade a jury.

Figure 3.1 displays our assignment to replace a collection of disparate warehouses with a single, computer-automated storage and distribution center.

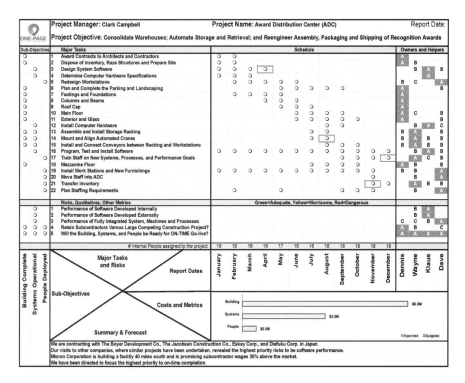

FIGURE 3.1   *The First OPPM Template*

Copyright OPPMi 2012. PDF color templates available at www.oppmi.com.

Comments from Readers and Users

The OPPM is a very concise way of reporting a lot of info in a very easy to understand single-page report. I'm looking forward to implementing this at DFW.
—R. Bee, Dallas Fort Worth Airport

Be careful when selecting your team. You want those who can execute and not just plan.

Efficient, effective, well-designed project management has just the right amount of details, while avoiding too many. Often, the more detailed and the more elegant the plan is, the more pedantic and the more plodding the execution becomes. To put it bluntly, you can be too obsessive about project processes. The details can become the drivers, and when this happens, you lose sight of what's important and the management process becomes ineffective. Eventually, the project breaks down and fails. To use a cliché, you can't see the forest for the trees. Moreover, senior management does not need, nor want, to know all the details.

 One of the strengths of OPPM, which may be counterintuitive, is that it has just the right degree of the absence of precision.

The first project in which we used this tool involved the building of a $10 million award distribution center at our headquarters in Salt Lake City. Computerized cranes had to be shipped from Japan to Salt Lake City, and whether they would arrive on time was a source of considerable concern to the project team. Part of that concern was because of the distance involved, but part was because of a devastating earthquake that hit Kobe, Japan, on January 17, 1995, one month into the yearlong project. The earthquake affected numerous distribution channels through which the crane components were arriving.

Management needed to know if this equipment would arrive on time, if this process was on budget, and who was responsible for making sure this happened, but it didn't need to know the details of how the cranes made their way to Salt Lake City from Japan and all the effort that had to be expended to make sure the right equipment arrived at the right time.

K E Y CONCEPT The OPPM navigates between failing to plan and overplanning. The plan is just the beginning—the means to the end, but not the end.

The OPPM showed our stakeholders how the crane aspect of this project was progressing but not every detail behind this part of the project. Senior management, by using the OPPM, received detailed, but not overly detailed, information. The information was presented in a quick, easily understood, easily digestible format. Project task owners know and manage the details—senior management doesn't need, nor want, to know these details. These owners also know that management is watching their performance.

K E Y CONCEPT The OPPM makes a project's owners readily identifiable to every stakeholder. An experienced project manager in one of Mick's courses noted, "It telegraphs my team and their tasks to those most interested."

The OPPM makes clear—visually, through the use of interconnected graphics and color—who is responsible for what and how each person is performing. Senior management sees, immediately by glancing at one page, who is performing well and who is behind on his or her portion of the project.

Not only does this visualization make it easier for management to understand a project's status and who is responsible, but it also is an important motivator to the owners. They are clearly aware that their role and performance are continually and immediately visible.

Comments from Readers and Users

The most valuable component was The One-Page Project Manager template with a focus on how simple communication is key to successful project management.

—K. Shuler, Cisco

CONCEPT

The OPPM is a tool that can be used in a surprisingly wide array of projects.

Its first use was for a construction project, but at O.C. Tanner, we've also used it for the following:

- Implementing a software project: an enterprise resource planning (ERP) project using SAP software that cost $30 million
- Launching a new Internet business: Entrada, which provides performance awards that companies give to their top-performing employees
- Obtaining ISO 9000 certification

- Addressing a long-standing problem: an accounts receivable reduction project that decreased accounts receivable by almost a full month
- Winning a prize: the Shingo Prize, an award given for excellence in manufacturing; O.C. Tanner won it in 1999

Thousands of projects have been planned and corresponding status reports have been generated on OPPMs over the past 17 years. Examples in this book reflect a "progressive elaboration" and a continuing refinement of the basic architecture of the OPPM.

The OPPM can also clarify your thinking and provide unexpected benefits. For example, in our project to reduce accounts receivable, the OPPM revealed that of the four processes involved with accounts receivables, the process of generating invoices had no owner. As a result, it was out of control. Knowing this, we were quickly able to assign an owner to this part of the process, the process was brought under control, and accounts receivable balances were significantly reduced.

 The OPPM doesn't replace your existing tools; it augments what you are already using. It is important to emphasize this point strongly. If you use Microsoft Project, then continue! If you drive projects with Primavera, continue! Many organizations that successfully use those comprehensive software tools are simply resting the OPPM "on top" as an executive status

report. Referring back to our watch metaphor, computer tools, like the cogs and jewels of the watch movement, deliver the results; the OPPM communicates the results.

The information presented in the OPPM isn't new. What's new is that existing information is placed in a format that is easy to read and to use. That's not a trivial distinction.

 An argument could be made that the success of projects is enhanced and improved through the use of the OPPM.

Comments from Readers and Users

Project Managers became necessary as project complexity grew. Then project management itself became too complex to explain project status to the stakeholders. OPPM cuts through the rhetoric and gives you the tools to easily bring about stakeholder understanding of the product, process, and status of every open project.

—J. Hoffman, GMRC

Before moving on to building and reporting by using the OPPM, a few comments comparing traditional with agile project management will be helpful. And of course, we need a visual.

Figure 3.2 shows the basic similarities between traditional and agile project components.

- Each makes progress over time toward a vision.
- Each requires cost and resources.
- Each strives for higher quality and lower risk.

Figure 3.3 reveals that the processes and the approach differentiate these two powerful project methodologies. Suppose the traditional triangle on the left represents a project to build a Boeing 737 aircraft. The 737 entered airline service in 1968 and is the best-selling jet airliner in the

Traditional & Agile Project Management
Basic Similarities

FIGURE 3.2   *Traditional and Agile Project Management, Basic Similarities*
Copyright OPPMi 2012.

history of aviation, with more than 7,000 aircraft delivered and more than 2,000 on order as of April 2012. The vision is clear, we know exactly what we want, and the plan for delivering the value includes the whole vision. Engineering specifications are clear, supply chains are well defined, production costs are precisely known, and manufacturing times are defined and documented. Quality is built in to the process with operational excellence, and the acceptable parameters for risk reducing tests are standardized.

We know what we want, how long it takes, how much it will cost, and how to guarantee high quality with the lowest risk. And, we release a completely finished aircraft, capable and ready to fly.

Now let's suppose that the triangle on the right of Figure 3.3 represents the agile approach to designing and

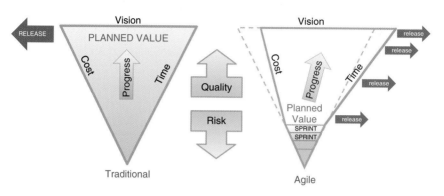

Traditional & Agile Project Management
Process and Approach Differences

FIGURE 3.3   *Traditional and Agile Project Management, Process and Approach Differences*
Copyright OPPMi 2012.

deploying a new in-dash GPS system for New York's fleet of taxicabs. We have a fixed budget and a highly publicized date, 24 weeks away, when the mayor plans to announce the new upgrade.

We have the high-level outline of a vision, yet there is disagreement among various stakeholders on which features are most important. We have selected 20 cabs into which we will place the latest release of our GPS every six weeks. We will plan and deliver it in three 2-week sprints prior to each of four releases. Each release will provide fully working software for a minimally marketable set of features. We will set and reset feature backlogs and priorities along the way by working with cab drivers, customers, and other stakeholders.

As we progress through each sprint and release, we will be adjusting our vision as priorities are repositioned, technology is refined, and learning is acquired by our development team. When the mayor presents the newly equipped taxis to the city in six months, he declares the project on time and on budget, with a final vision a little different than was originally presumed, acknowledging that quality was addressed and improved in each iteration. He is aware of the reduced risks of missing the delivery date of his announcement or exceeding the budget, while continually surpassing stakeholders' expectations, even though those expectations are quite different at project completion than they were in the beginning.

We will now explore OPPMs for both traditional and agile projects.

A Traditional Project

FIVE ESSENTIAL PARTS OF A PROJECT

The Project Management Institute provides a 5-by-9 construct for thinking about projects—42 separate processes are each aligned with one of five process groups and one of nine knowledge areas. The Harvard Pocket Mentor outlines a simpler approach by proposing four phases for every project. Our experience is that every traditional project has five essential parts:

- Tasks: the how
- Objectives: the what and the why
- Timeline: the when
- Cost: the how much
- Owners: the who

Communicating each element is necessary, which is why we have used these traditional elements as the structure of the one-page project manager (OPPM). (See Figure 4.1.)

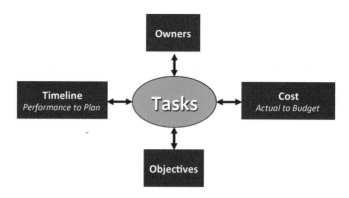

FIGURE 4.1   *Five Essential Elements of a Traditional Project*
Copyright OPPMi 2012.

Let's look at these five elements in more detail:

1. **Tasks: the how**—Tasks are the center of a project and need to be completed to accomplish the objectives. They are about the nuts and bolts of a project, the specifics of how it needs to be done. The hierarchy and interdependencies of tasks are part of the work breakdown structure.

2. **Objectives: the what and the why**—The purpose of a project is its vision. Ken Blanchard, in his book *The Heart of a Leader* (Tulsa, OK: Eagle Publishing, 2002) writes, "Knowing where you are going is the first stop in getting there." A project's objectives can be general or specific but are always measured by whether they are done on time and on budget.

3. **Timeline: the when**—When things are supposed to be done (and when they are actually done) are monitored on the timeline. If you expand a project scope, you have to expand the time or the

money allotted. "Time is a versatile performer. It flies, marches on, heals all wounds, runs out, and will tell," writes Franklin P. Jones, as quoted in *Wise Words and Quotes* (Colorado Springs, CO: Tyndale House, 2000) by Vernon McLellan.

4. **Cost: the how much**—Some costs are capitalized, such as building materials, requiring cash now and affecting income through future depreciation. Project expenses, reflected in the income statement, can be hard costs, such as consulting, or soft costs, as with internal staff deployed on the project. Cost accounting can be complicated, and large projects need input from accounting professionals.

5. **Owners: the who**—These are those who have accepted responsibility and are committed to delivering the objective.

The OPPM helps people who are involved in the project to think and act like owners.

Ownership transparency tends to positively affect personal engagement. It engages those involved in a project. As they see how their part of a project is progressing, they know that others see how well they are performing: ownership is a key to engagement. Full engagement requires both heart and mind:

• **Heart**: An appreciation for and commitment to a project's vision, complete with a clear understanding about what you own, engages the heart. Documentation and display of ownership magnifies this understanding and commitment. When the owner knows that colleagues, senior management, or others know about this ownership, the owner's emotional engagement with a project deepens.

- **Mind** : The OPPM provides a clear connection between ownership and the project's objectives and metrics. The mind portion of project management involves showing what the participants own and how objectives are measured.

Clear ownership illuminates performance, highlighting those who deserve to be recognized and receive commendations for jobs well done and those who need to be assisted. The OPPM makes it easier to be sure those who deserve recognition receive it because the major owners of a project are listed on the tool. This isn't trivial because appreciation for great work accelerates performance, yet senior management often doesn't know whom to reward or appreciate. Senior managers often get their information from sound bites—comments from managers or others, things they hear, or feelings they have about a person or a piece of the project. This can cause overrewarding the undeserving or underappreciating those who perform well.

 With the OPPM, responsible owners are clearly manifest.

OWNERSHIP IS REMARKABLY POWERFUL

The following five cases exemplify how ownership generates engagement and often some unexpected accomplishments.

Shingo Prize Project

We had one month to submit our application for the Shingo Prize. Senior management didn't think we could do it. I invited anyone in the company who wanted to help to join the team. They would not earn any extra money, and the work would be done after hours. The team, in fact, worked from 5:00 PM to midnight for a month to complete this project. They understood the vision; were energized by the thought of beating the odds; and were welded together by a single, time-constrained focus. It was an invigorated and eager team, and it created an emotional and productive climate. You can keep a team on that level of commitment for only a short time. We did it for one month, and we brought home the prize—literally and metaphorically. I subsequently served on the Shingo Board of Governors. This intense involvement with lean practices and operational excellence led, in part, to the third OPPM book, *The One-Page Project Manager for Execution: Drive Strategy & Solve Problems with a Single Sheet of Paper*.

Boiler Stack

As we were building our award distribution center, we discovered late in the project that building codes required the boiler stack to extend 5 feet above the building. This would mean an ugly, tall, wired-down, galvanized stack rising above our beautiful building. To reroute it would cost $100,000, which wasn't in the budget. The owner of that part of the project took it on himself to find a solution. He ferreted out an obscure opportunity. If a blower was installed in the stack, the code said the stack didn't have to extend beyond the roofline and, with a little paint, he could almost hide this unplanned distraction. For $10,000, a workable solution involving a blower was found. This employee had a personal, emotional connection because he had a great deal of ownership in this project. This ownership came about because his name was on the OPPM connected to this part of the project—and the objective to complete the project within budget.

ISO 9000

We hired consultants to help us get the coveted ISO 9000 international certification and therefore had both internal owners and external consultant owners. The ownership elements of OPPM resulted in unexpected and valuable consequences for our consultants and us. We will explore this in detail in Chapter 12. Alamo Learning Systems and its president, Guy Hale, provided expert guidance, assisting us to successfully complete this project in five months rather than the expected six.

Accounts Receivable Project

For years, our accounts receivable were too high. Previous attempts to resolve this problem would push responsibility down to the collections department. We set up a formal project, complete with an OPPM; on that tool, we placed the names of sales vice presidents. After all, it was the sales department that generated all these accounts receivable, and a sale really isn't a sale until the money is collected. This got the attention of the right people, and once they took ownership, major changes occurred. This, combined with assigning an owner to the setup, invoicing, and collecting processes, resulted in a reduction of unpaid accounts by 29 percent.

Enterprise Resource Planning Project

Lest you think that the OPPM is a cure-all, a guarantee that all projects will be highly successful, let me tell you about an enterprise resource planning (ERP) project we did at O.C. Tanner. We delivered it on budget and it had the return on investment promised, but it was not delivered on time. Actually, it took more than twice as long as originally forecast. However, management was able to accommodate this schedule because it knew, as the project progressed, why the project was running late and by how much. It knew this because every two weeks it received an updated OPPM that clearly showed which aspects of the project were falling behind the desired timeline and which were on time. The OPPM could not, by itself, bring this project in on time, but it could communicate to management what was happening, where the difficulties were, who was responsible, and what to expect. It was by shifting from traditional to agile project management methods that this project eventually met timing expectations. We will explore this in the agile OPPM Chapters 7, 8, and 9.

CONCEPT OPPM helps everyone avoid surprises, and when managing a project, you don't want surprises.

Our experience has been that status reports for both traditional and agile projects tend toward the traditional. A pure agile practitioner would encourage interested stakeholders, including management, to personally come to the team room where status information "radiates" from dynamic displays on most every wall. Such communication visits should happen, but often they do not. And status reports are required, often in a format familiar to management. Many traditional OPPMs are at this very moment being used to communicate status on both agile and traditional projects.

Figure 4.2 shows how the five essential parts fit into a standard X-chart. This is the basic skeleton of a traditional OPPM.

The Matrix

Figure 4.3 is the traditional OPPM basic template. Toward the bottom left-hand corner, a rectangle is divided into

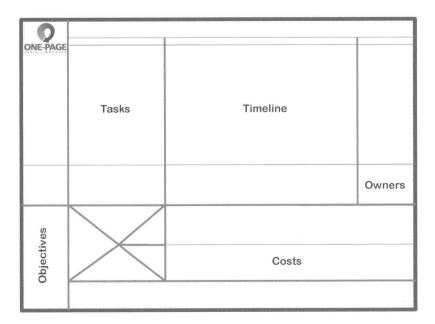

FIGURE 4.2   *The OPPM X-Chart*
Copyright OPPMi 2012. PDF color templates available at www.oppmi.com.

five unequal pie-like pieces. This rectangle represents the heart of the OPPM. We call it the matrix—the point where all the elements of the OPPM—and project management in general—come together. As you become familiar with the OPPM, you'll see that its various elements all flow to this rectangle.

Major Tasks and Risks

The section of the matrix labeled Major Tasks and Risks is depicted in the column directly above it and is in two parts: the top, which has the heading Major Tasks, lists the project's major tasks, and the section below has the heading Risks, Qualitatives, Other Metrics.

45

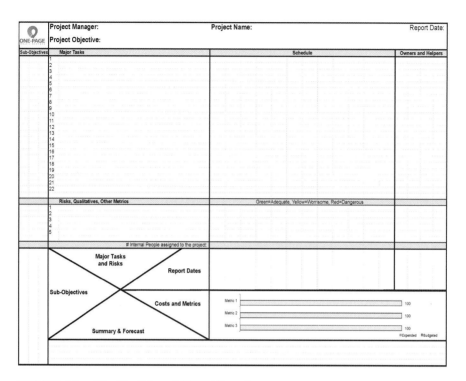

FIGURE 4.3   *The Traditional OPPM Template*

Copyright OPPMi 2012. PDF color templates available at www.oppmi.com.

Think of the top section as a list of quantitative measures, whereas the bottom section depicts qualitative aspects of a project.

Under Major Tasks, the number you list depends on the project and how detailed you want to be, all supported by your project work breakdown structure. But be aware that too many tasks minimize the effectiveness of the OPPM, making it clumsy and overwhelming. Plus, you have only one page for everything. Include too many tasks, and you won't fit everything on the one page.

In the example shown here, we have room for 22 major project tasks. Even for very large projects, this is usually enough; smaller projects will have fewer tasks. Shortly, I'll walk you through the building of an actual OPPM, and you'll see how the task portion of the tool is developed.

Keep in mind that behind each of these tasks, there could be another OPPM, Microsoft Project, Gantt charts, or PERT (program evaluation and review technique) charts. Let's say you are constructing a building, and the OPPM with the topmost view, the one seen by highest management, has as a major task the construction of the foundation. On one line of the form you could write, "constructing foundation." That task could then have its own OPPM that covers the major tasks involved with constructing the foundation, such as digging the hole, constructing supports, and pouring the concrete. Each of these could have its own OPPM, and so forth.

KEY CONCEPT Projects are all about getting things done, about turning activities into results. Ultimately, projects are not about activities but about successfully completing tasks.

Tasks are really the centerpiece of any project—the heart of the OPPM. Constructing a building involves many different tasks, and ideally, those tasks are done correctly, on time and on budget.

Risks, Qualitatives, Other Metrics

Risk mitigation and some key performance indicators are qualitative by nature. They are a matter of judgment. They are listed in the Risk, Qualitatives, Other Metrics section and will be reported on with traffic light colors: green, yellow, and red.

Report Dates and Schedule

Moving clockwise around the matrix, we next come to the section labeled Report Dates. These are the dates the boss wants in status reports. The schedule is laid out in the large section resting above the set of report dates.

Costs and Metrics

We use a simple bar chart in the open box to the right of the Costs and Metrics triangle. Usually a set of double bars extends across the page, one for the budget and one for actual expenses. Costs are plotted as the project progresses.

Summary & Forecast

Write notes about aspects of the project not covered by the other sectors of the OPPM in the Summary & Forecast section. Stakeholders want to know "Why?" and "What's next?"

KEY CONCEPT The Summary & Forecast space is limited. That's by design. It forces the project manager to think and write succinctly. Remember, "serious simplicity." Never reiterate in the Summary & Forecast what is already illustrated on the OPPM. Focus on explaining deviations from plan, together with a forecast of remedies. Knowing what you now know, give management your newly informed view of how the project will appear by the completion of the next two or three time boxes.

Sub-Objectives

The objective of the project is spelled out at the top of the OPPM. The sub-objectives are a high-level breakdown of the major project deliverables. Sub-objectives must be measurable and verifiable. They are the desired results of the project, and as you can see on the OPPM, they are tied to the various tasks. However, not every sub-objective is tied to every task.

For example, a construction project might have its objective "the consolidation and reengineering of certain corporate functions." The sub-objectives tied to each task would be "Building Complete," "Systems Operational," and "People Deployed." One task would be "Columns and beams erected." That could be tied to the "Building Complete" sub-objective. Another task could be the installation of certain software. The sub-objective tied to this would be "System Operational." The task of software user training is tied to "People Deployed."

Constructing the OPPM

You now know the basics of the matrix, so let's get started on how to construct an OPPM. I've broken down the process into 12 bite-sized pieces that can be altered and changed to meet whatever project you are working on:

1. Header
2. Owners
3. Matrix
4. Project sub-objectives
5. Major tasks

6. Aligning tasks to sub-objectives

7. Report dates

8. Aligning tasks to report dates

9. Aligning tasks and schedule to owners

10. Risks, qualitatives and other metrics

11. Costs and metrics

12. Summary and forecast

O.C. Tanner is in the business of creating and distributing various types of employee awards—recognition, performance, and safety, among others. Figure 4.4 and all of the figures in Chapters 5 and 6 are from the project we called the Award Distribution Center (ADC).

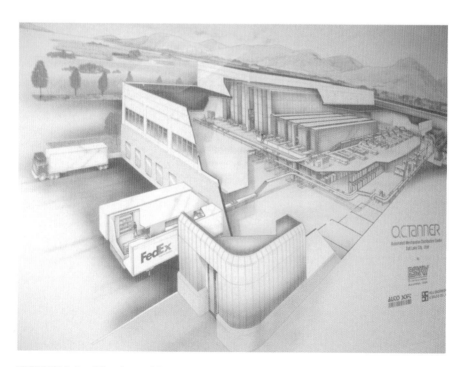

FIGURE 4.4   *The Award Distribution Center, Traditional OPPM*
Copyright OPPMi 2012.

50

In the first edition of this book, I used the OPPM that we used during the construction of the ADC. But just as project management is a technique that is continually improved, so is the OPPM. Since I first wrote about the OPPM, as a result of my own experience with it and the experience of thousands of users who have used the tool with tens of thousands of projects and have been gracious enough to give Mick and me their feedback and tell us of their experiences, the OPPM has been refined—not dramatically, but in subtle and productive ways.

In this book, we will refer to these updated OPPMs as they relate to the ADC and other projects as if they were in place at the time of the projects. If interested in the OPPMs in their original context, please see this book's first edition.

The ADC (Figure 4.4) is a building we constructed that is dominated by an automated storage and retrieval system (ASRS). Found between the rows are shelves with robotic carriers that run on tracks and can pick out one award at a time out of the tens of thousands of awards we inventory at any given moment. They also can restock the shelves. The stocking and retrieving of our awards inventory is entirely automatic.

The project manager and the project's owners and helpers fill in the OPPM. They construct it, and then it becomes the basis for their status reports.

The OPPM must be a team effort; your team consists of all the task owners. You may have to negotiate with team members, but, ultimately, you need buy-in and consensus from your team.

The 12 Construction Steps for a Traditional OPPM

The location of all 12 construction steps are shown at the top of the completed one-page project manager (OPPM) in Figure 5.1. When an OPPM is finished, we present it for project approval and funding. Figure 5.1 provides the opportunity for you to "begin with the end in mind."

Now let's create an OPPM.

STEP 1: THE HEADER

What It Is

The first step is to provide basic information about the project. This goes at the top of the form in the highlighted rectangle (Figure 5.2).

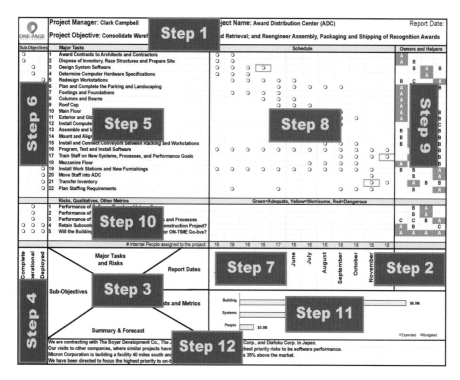

FIGURE 5.1 *The 12 OPPM Construction Steps*

Copyright OPPMi 2012. PDF color templates available at www.oppmi.com.

The following sections are included:

- Project Name
- Project Manager
- Project Objective
- Report Date

How to Do It

Project Name: Award Distribution Center (ADC)

In our example, the name given the project is purely descriptive—Award Distribution Center (ADC). Naming the project sounds simple, and to some degree it

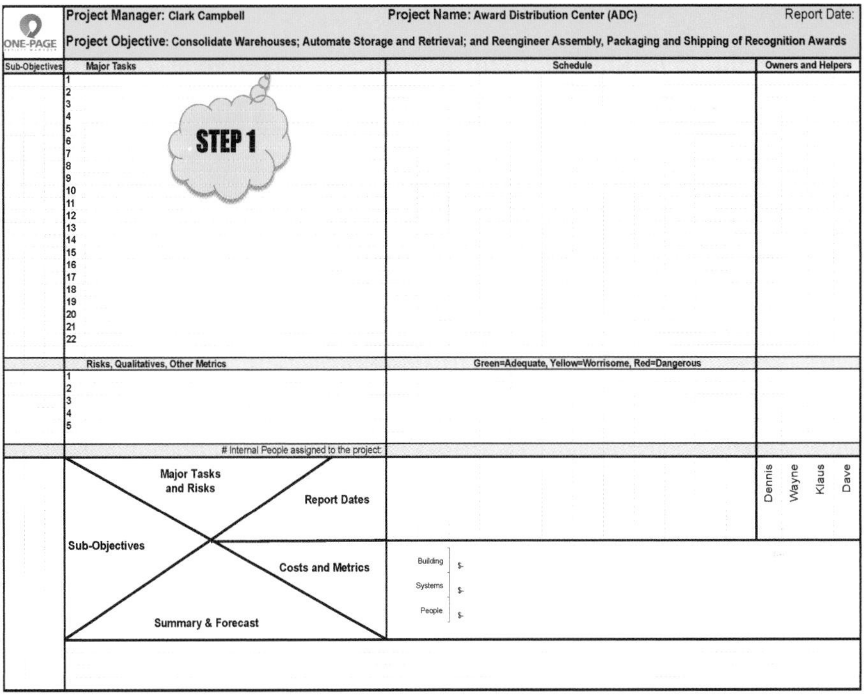

Sub-Objectives	Major Tasks	Schedule	Owners and Helpers

Project Manager: Clark Campbell   **Project Name:** Award Distribution Center (ADC)   Report Date:

Project Objective: Consolidate Warehouses; Automate Storage and Retrieval; and Reengineer Assembly, Packaging and Shipping of Recognition Awards

ONE-PAGE

STEP 1

1 2 3 4 5 6 7 8 9 10 11 12 13 14 15 16 17 18 19 20 21 22

Risks, Qualitatives, Other Metrics	Green=Adequate, Yellow=Worrisome, Red=Dangerous

1 2 3 4 5

Internal People assigned to the project:

Major Tasks and Risks

Report Dates

Sub-Objectives

Costs and Metrics

Building $-
Systems $-
People $-

Summary & Forecast

Dennis Wayne Klaus Dave

FIGURE 5.2   *Step 1: The Header*

Copyright OPPMi 2012. PDF color templates available at www.oppmi.com.

is. But don't take this task lightly. The name you give will be in front of everyone involved with the project every day, as well as those looking at the project (such as senior management). For this reason, having the objective of the project be part of the name is often a good idea (for example, Reducing Accounts Receivable Project—not Reengineering Project #2; Winning Shingo Prize Project—not Manufacturing Excellence Award). Using the name to subtly reinforce the purpose of the project to participants day after day has value.

When naming the project, recognize the power of language. Apollo Project, the United States' project to reach the moon, made for a great sound bite, which is why it was such an effective project name. The Titanic Project, however, probably would send the wrong message. Don't get too cute with a project's name, but a catchy title can help engage people and have the project stand out among many projects.

You might want to hold off naming the project until you have your team in place. Then, together, everyone can contribute to the project's name.

Project Manager: Clark Campbell

I was assigned to lead this project. Each project must, ultimately, have one owner, one project manager. This person's name is the one that goes at the top of the OPPM. Everyone who reads the form knows who is ultimately in charge of and responsible for the project.

In Step 1, the executive in charge must be identified. Let me be clear: this person must be the one in charge. This cannot be an advisor, a consultant, or anyone who is not a full-time employee of your organization.

We won't go into great detail about the abilities needed by the project manager, but because we are addressing the issue of communication, we should be clear that this manager has to be an excellent communicator.

I've divided the communications skills needed by project managers into three types:

- **Up:** This is communication that goes from the person up the hierarchy to upper levels of supervision and management.

- **Down:** This is communication that goes from the person down the hierarchy to subordinates.
- **Out:** This is communication that goes from the person out to his or her associates, colleagues, and peers. In the organization's hierarchy, these are folks at the same level as the project manager. This communication also reaches out to stakeholders beyond the organization.

Most people are not equally adept at all forms of communication. Some are very competent and comfortable in the president's office; they are good at up communication. Others work well with their peers but are uncomfortable when dealing with the board of directors. Still others are good at motivating their team but don't know how to communicate well with supervisors or how to interact well with peers.

Every project manager needs to be good at straight talk. This is talk that is honest, complete, and to the point and that addresses issues you might otherwise not wish to discuss. If your project is in trouble, you need to say so—don't cover it up. If you're a bit worried, that too needs to be conveyed. Straight talk is not pessimism. It is honesty. If a piece of a project is behind schedule and other parts of the project are thereby being held up, the straight-talking project manager will acknowledge the problem, be honest about its consequences, and then devise a strategy that lets the project team continue where it can be productive, while assisting the behind-schedule part of the project to catch up. This is honest optimism and is saying, "We can do this or that and help the project along" while acknowledging the problems and challenges.

TiP Never hide critical issues from management or your team. Why? (1) No one likes surprises, and (2) the help and support you get from others when they learn of your problems may pleasantly surprise you.

Here's an example of straight talk—and the lack thereof. I don't know if this story is true or apocryphal, but it doesn't matter. The message it sends is certainly accurate. Someone was planning a very large breakfast meeting and was talking to the caterer to see if the meeting was feasible, given certain requirements. The meeting planner asked if it would be possible to have the meeting at 6:00 AM. The caterer immediately said, "No problem." Next question: "We will have 500 people. Is that a problem?" The immediate response: "No problem." Next question: "We want to serve everyone an eight-ounce glass of orange juice. Is that a problem?" The immediate response: "No problem." The next question: "We want this orange juice to be freshly squeezed. Is that a problem?" The immediate response: "No problem." That's when the event planner knew he was in trouble. Squeezing 500 eight-ounce glasses of orange juice to be ready at 6:00 AM is a definite challenge. The caterer wasn't giving the event planner straight talk. He was shining over the challenges, hoping to win the business. A variation on this would be if the caterer had started complaining about squeezing all this fresh orange juice early in the morning and saying it couldn't be done. That's not straight talk either—that's a naysayer who is a pessimist and unwilling to "find a way."

What would a straight talker say? When asked if it was possible to serve 500 eight-ounce glasses of freshly squeezed orange juice first thing in the morning, he would say, "Let me think about that," take out his calculator, figure out how much orange juice was needed, how many oranges would have to be ordered and stored, and how many machines and people it would take to produce the desired amount of orange juice at the prescribed time. Then he would calculate the costs and quote a price. This is straight talk. It's not trying to avoid a situation or gloss over it. Instead, it is trying to meet the challenge in an honest and productive way. Project managers should always engage in straight talk. Management, peers, and project teams are drawn toward and engaged by straight talk.

TiP Project managers who avoid the words "No, but" know that the very same qualifying message can be far better prefaced by the words, "Yes, and."

I'm going into this detail about communication because, ultimately, the OPPM is a communication tool. As I have already noted, it was first designed to communicate to upper management—up communication. But over time we have found it effective at communicating out with those in the organization who have a stake in the project and down to those working on the project.

Project Objective: Consolidate Warehouses; Automate Storage and Retrieval; and Reengineer Assembly, Packaging, and Shipping of Recognition Awards

The same people who assigned the project in the first place usually give the project's objective to the project manager. If, as project manager, you are not given the project's objective, go back to those who gave you the project and get it. They need to know the project's objective. If they don't, you, they, and the project will all be in trouble. If they are unclear about the project's objective, here are a couple of questions to ask them that will help them focus on what the project is all about:

- What do you hope to achieve from the project?
- How should we measure progress?

When you have the project's objective, write it down. This allows everyone to see it and ensures everyone is in agreement. The objective of any project is the project's purpose, what you want to do, what you want to accomplish. "Gaining ISO 9000 Certification" could be both the name of a project and the objective of a project. Typically, the objective would be aimed at

- Creating . . .
- Completing . . .
- Implementing . . .

You need to write down the project's objective in just a few words. It should not be a paragraph, but rather a sentence or fragment of a sentence.

Defining the project's objective is not something you, the executive in charge of the project, can do in isolation, nor should it come from on high and be forced on those involved. The objective needs to be worked out by the stakeholders. These include the team members who will work on the project; senior management, which is providing funding for the project; and anyone else who will benefit from the project. If you don't involve the various stakeholders, there's a good chance you will try to achieve something the stakeholders don't want or won't accept because they had no say in the project's objective.

The first of Andy Crowe's Alpha Four is to collaborate early. Step 1 provides this opportunity. You, as project manager, will be making decisions and giving direction to your project. That often means making trade-offs. As part of completing the header, discuss with the boss your eventual need to make these trade-offs affecting cost, schedule, scope, quality, and risks. You and the boss must share a clear understanding of priorities. On-time completion of the ADC was most important to my boss, followed closely by cost. We then knew, for example, that when balancing schedule against scope, meeting our deadlines would take precedence.

STEP 2: THE OWNERS
What It Is

We'll assume from this point on you are the project manager because this is the person who typically puts the OPPM together (of course, with the help of the others on

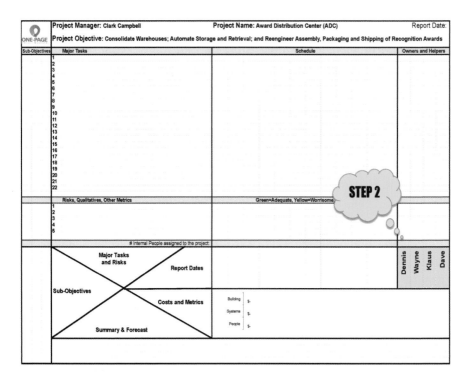

FIGURE 5.3   *Step 2: The Owners*

Copyright OPPMi 2012. PDF color templates available at www.oppmi.com.

the project team). Your next step is to list your team. Who will be working on the project? Who will be responsible for the parts of the project? These are the people who will manage the major components of the project and be instrumental to your success in managing the project. In Figure 5.3, the highlighted box along the right side has space for the names of the owners. Here is where you place the names of those on your immediate team. The owners are listed as Dennis, Wayne, Klaus, and Dave.

How to Do It

Your team will consist of owners and helpers. Owners are those with primary responsibility of each major task, whereas helpers are those with secondary or tertiary responsibility for each major task. We will link these owners to their specific tasks in Step 6.

Here are some pointers on how to name your team of owners and helpers. Of course, you must match people with the needs and requirements of the project. You'll have to consider each person's experience, knowledge, and skills—and how they fit the project's needs. And you should also consider personalities. How well do these people work together? If two people, for instance, are known to dislike one another, it doesn't mean they both cannot be on the team. It just means if you put them both on the team, you believe you can manage their differences and that the extra work of managing them is worth the benefits each brings to the overall project.

Also, keep the number of owners and helpers as small as possible. From my experience, three or four is usually about right. On larger projects, you'll have more than one layer of OPPMs, and each of these will have its own set of owners and helpers. Each OPPM should be limited to a handful of owners and helpers.

Let me say a few more words about the owners and helpers. The success of your project largely depends on them. If they're good, if they're engaged, if they're effective, and if they can execute and make things happen, chances are very high your project will be a success.

This is critical: your owners must be able to execute, to make things happen. If they can't, find new owners.

You, as the lead manager, must also know the amount of time your owners can contribute to the project. Are they working on it full time? If so, does their home department expect them to continue to do some of their original job function? When this happens, you have a potential problem, because these people are working more than one full-time job. If a person is supposed to work for your project one-quarter of the time, but his or her home department hasn't reduced any of the person's responsibilities during the life of the project, you face the same type of problem.

That said, recognize that the people involved with a project, especially a project that has generated a strong commitment from its owners and participants, often will find the time the project needs. They'll find a way to get the job done even though, as project owners, they typically do not get any additional compensation or relief from some of their nonproject responsibilities for the work they do on the project.

TIP Getting part of a star employee's time can prove more valuable than getting all of the time of an employee who is a moderate performer. Keep this in mind when choosing your team.

Also, as a group you'd do well to have the owners represent a variety of viewpoints, and not just view things similarly among them. You might want a realist, a skeptic, and a Pollyanna-type person. Each has strengths and weaknesses, but together they can make a formidable team capable of handling a variety of obstacles and challenges.

STEP 3: THE MATRIX

What It Is

Earlier I talked about the matrix. Think of this as the hub, the focal point, and the intersection where all points meet. Or, to use another metaphor, think of it as a compass that will guide your project from start to finish. As you'll see in Figure 5.4, this is the step where you reference the matrix while in conversation with your team. The matrix provides the foundation for the entire OPPM and links all of a project's essential elements. It communicates these elements to your readers.

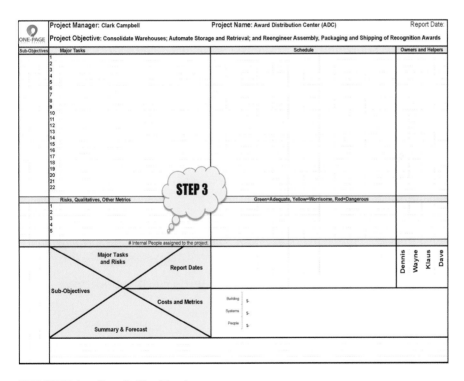

FIGURE 5.4   *Step 3: The Matrix*

Copyright OPPMi 2012. PDF color templates available at www.oppmi.com.

How to Do It

In this step you will gather your team and start the discussion of how to handle this project. You'll present an overview of the project to your team and, in rough outline, discuss the pieces of the matrix, including sub-objectives, major project tasks and risks, report dates, and costs and metrics. Admittedly, the matrix, and the OPPM in general, is a rather simplified way of looking at a project. But that's one of its strengths—it does not try to do everything involved with a project. It just takes the pieces of information of most interest and value to upper management and others and presents them in a format that's quickly and easily followed and understood. That's its strength, and the matrix is where all the important steps of the OPPM converge.

During Step 3, the project manager tutors each team member on how to build and use the OPPM. This step is also a reminder for you to ensure that each team member also receives the necessary general project management training sufficient for the unique demands of the specific project.

TiP You will find that as you and your staff struggle through completing the 12 steps, a team will come together. You will experience a growing competence and confidence in your joint ability to successfully complete your assigned project—together.

STEP 4: THE SUB-OBJECTIVES
What It Is

With the team now in place, you and your team start to break down the project into sub-objectives, so called because they are subordinate to the project's overall objective (such as constructing a building or reducing accounts receivable). As Harold Kerzner notes in *Project Management*, the characteristics of project sub-objectives must be

- Specific, not general
- Not overly complex
- Measurable, tangible, and verifiable
- Of an appropriate level; challenging
- Realistic and attainable
- Established within resource bounds
- Consistent with resources available or anticipated
- Consistent with organizational plans, policies, and procedures

The sub-objectives go in the rectangle on the lower left-hand corner of the OPPM, which is highlighted in Figure 5.5. For the ADC, they are Building Complete (completing the construction of the building), Systems Operational (meaning that all the computer and mechanical systems within the building are operational and working the way they were specified to work), and People Deployed (all the people who will be working

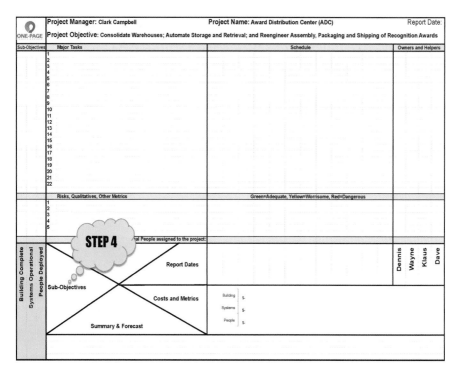

FIGURE 5.5   *Step 4: The Sub-Objectives*

Copyright OPPMi 2012. PDF color templates available at www.oppmi.com.

in the distribution center are hired, trained on the new equipment, and ready to have the center up and running).

How to Do It

You need to break the project down into sub-objectives, and these typically number no more than three to five. As with the number of owners and the use of the OPPM, we are on a quest for simplicity. The $10 million ADC we built at O.C. Tanner had only three sub-objectives attached to the project: Building Complete, Systems Operational, and People Deployed.

You need to ask yourself and your team: What's really important with this project? Is being on time really vital? Is cutting costs important? What do you really need to achieve with this project?

Every competent project manager knows he or she must balance three project variables or constraints of a project, each dependent on the other:

1. **Time:** This refers to the time required for the various steps involved with a project and ultimately the time it takes to complete the entire project.

2. **Resources:** These are the assets you have at your disposal to complete the project. Usually, the most important resources are people and money.

3. **Scope:** Paula Martin and Karen Tate, in their book *Project Management Memory Jogger,* 2nd ed. (Salem, NH: Goal/QPC, 2010), provide this definition of *scope*: "The project scope defines who the customers are, the final deliverables that will be produced for them, and the criteria that the customers will use to judge their satisfaction with the deliverables" (p. 53).

How do these three factors play a role in project management? They work together, and when one gets out of balance, the entire project can come tumbling down. To prevent that, you, the project manager, have to make adjustments in the other two factors.

For example, say you were building a house for you and your family. If you have a mortgage and can't add any more to the down payment, the money you are working with is fixed. In that case, if you want to, say, add a bathroom to the house, something else will have to give, perhaps the size of the master bedroom or the number of closets. You have to adjust one variable to accommodate a change in another. Balance and equilibrium must be maintained.

TIP When determining your objectives, find a few that are a litmus test for your project. What are the major accomplishments you want to achieve? When you can answer this question, determining the project's objectives will prove relatively easy.

One of the benefits of creating an OPPM is that, as you work through it, you gain an increasing understanding of the project, and you and your team will discover, through this process, those aspects of the project that will need the majority of your attention and those that are less critical.

Some objectives are so obvious they don't need to be enumerated on the OPPM, such as being on time and on budget. The three sub-objectives on the OPPM that we just discussed (Building Complete, Systems Operational, and People Deployed) were all discussed by and agreed to by the team. They're not profound, unexpected, or difficult to comprehend, which is why they are good objectives. They are simple, direct, to the point, easily understood, and, of course, valued. They really are, at their most basic, what this project is about.

STEP 5: THE MAJOR TASKS

What It Is

In Figure 5.6, you'll see highlighted on the left side of the OPPM a rectangle that encompasses the major project tasks. Of all the components of the OPPM, this is arguably the most important. Think of the tasks as what it will take to finish the project. A $10 million project is really just the sum total of fifty $200,000 projects or ten $1 million projects that are coordinated and combined to add up to the final project.

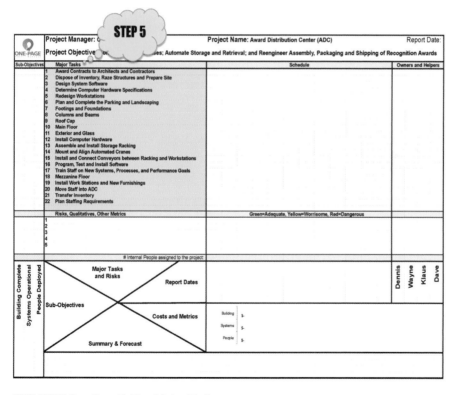

FIGURE 5.6   *Step 5: The Major Tasks*

Copyright OPPMi 2012. PDF color templates available at www.oppmi.com.

Project management professionals recognize this effort as the work breakdown structure (WBS). Eric Verzuh in Chapter 6 of his book, *The Fast Forward MBA in Project Management*, presents the WBS fundamentals clearly and completely.

The 22 major tasks we identified as a team are listed. These include from task 1, Award Contracts to Architects and Contractor, to task 22, Plan Staffing Requirements.

TiP To be effective, each task must be of a manageable size, where the scope is of a size that one person can be the lead.

How to Do It

With the OPPM, you take a large task, such as constructing a building, and break that down into smaller ones, such as award contracts, site demolition, and so on. In the case of the distribution center, the smaller tasks each appear on the highest-level OPPM, the one we are focusing on in this book. Each of these smaller tasks—Award Contracts . . . , Install Computer Hardware, Train Staff . . . , and so on—would, in turn, have its own OPPM or be supported by other project management software.

For large projects, you need to align your tasks with those shown in the project management software programs necessary for various parts of your project. The building aspects of our project were carefully detailed using the program Primavera P3. The software and hardware components were thoroughly constructed in Microsoft Project. The OPPM does not replace these often necessary and valuable tools. It "sits on top" as the highest-level learning, coordinating and then communicating document. Often, with smaller projects, you and your team don't need such help and can identify the tasks yourselves.

KEY CONCEPT You absolutely need buy-in from all participants. This is especially true for the tasks you delineate in the OPPM. Each task will be assigned at least one owner, and if owners and their teams are not in agreement with what is specified on the OPPM, the project is in jeopardy. Be sure to seek input and buy-in from owners, others inside the organization, outside consultants, and anyone else with a stake in the project.

In this book, we're focusing on the topmost level, the OPPM that would be looked at by senior management. Let's take the Reducing Accounts Receivable project I mentioned earlier. A task might be written as "the analysis of studying the creditworthiness of customers." If your customers aren't credit worthy, chances are you will have trouble collecting your accounts receivable. We might have an OPPM just for the task of analyzing the creditworthiness of customers. It would have its own task breakdown. This is what I mean by having multiple layers of OPPMs.

KEY CONCEPT In addition to being of manageable size, each task should be distinct—separate from other tasks. You can't have accountability if it is hard to tell where one task ends and another begins.

Constructing a building gets the topmost OPPM, and constructing the footings and foundations would be a task listed on this OPPM and could get its own OPPM. On the footings and foundations level, there might be a task involving building the wood forms needed to pour the concrete into. Constructing the foundation would be a distinct task on the topmost OPPM, and constructing the forms would be a distinct task on the OPPM that is just for the building's foundation.

 Tasks should be measurable in terms of their progress so that you can gauge their advancement and report on them in the OPPM.

Also, for the purpose of communication to stakeholders, you need enough such tasks, but not too many. Too many makes it hard to track what's going on and to get the big picture, whereas too few makes each task harder to see.

How many tasks are not too many but enough? A good rule is to try to average two to three tasks per reporting period for the length of the project. If the project will run nine months, 18 or so tasks are probably right. A two-year project would have approximately 48 tasks. On the other end of the spectrum, don't divide the project into too few tasks.

As I've noted before, communication is the key to project management and defining the major project tasks. Creating these definitions should be a team effort; one person—you or anyone else—should not dictate them. As the project is discussed, you and your team will probably get a sense of what the reasonable task divisions are. As with the name of the project, it's probably best to hold off for a while defining the tasks until you and your team get a good understanding of what's involved.

One reason this step is so critical is it involves not just the tasks but also the owners and helpers. As you create tasks, you have to align them with the project's owners and helpers. If one owner is particularly strong in one area, say financial controls, and the others are particularly weak in this area, then the financial person will likely take on many or most tasks involving finances. But if a number of tasks involve finances, this person may not be able to take them all on. In this case, some tasks with relatively minor financial control aspects to them might be given to some of the other owners or helpers, whereas the bulk of the financially oriented tasks go to the team member who knows about finances. What you've done here is align the tasks with owners and helpers. We will discuss this in Step 9.

CONTINUOUS IMPROVEMENT

Before we go further, let me take a detour to discuss a couple of important points.

When building the OPPM, it's always fair to revisit earlier steps. This tool is not carved in stone but is iterative. If, as the project progresses, you find the need to change something or tweak something else, do so. Be open to continual improvement. The OPPM is a tool designed to help you communicate aspects of a project to those with interests in the project. It is not something that should dictate how a project progresses or is managed.

 Bend the tool to fit the project, not the project to fit the tool.

The OPPM offers you one page to write all the information you need to convey. That's not much space, which I consider one of its advantages. It forces you to be descriptive, efficient, and precise with your language.

Avoid jargon, acronyms, and abbreviations. Keep in mind this OPPM will have to communicate up, down, and out, and not all of those audiences know the entire lingo you and your colleagues know. If you want to use this tool to its maximum effectiveness as a means to communicate, use language and a vocabulary everyone understands.

Accept the fact you don't have much space to be explanatory. View that as an advantage, as something that will help you communicate better. The very act of having to be so brief in your descriptions usually makes you more exacting. Your communications should improve with your using the OPPM.

One more thing: because the OPPM is one page, it cannot show all aspects of a project and is not designed to do so. That means important aspects of project management are not represented by this tool, perhaps most notably dependencies and capacity planning. If task 7 is dependent on the completion of task 4, you won't know this from the OPPM. The capacity of the system to deal with scarcity of resources—for example, there are an insufficient number of people available to do a task—will also not be represented in the tool. Owners must take responsibility for getting all the resources they need.

What's important here is acknowledging the limitations of the tool. It cannot depict everything about a project. Yet, its one page conveys virtually all the pertinent information that senior management needs to know about a project (up communication), much of the information of interest to peers (out communication), while providing an important bird's-eye view to those at lower levels (down communication).

STEP 6: ALIGNING TASKS WITH SUB-OBJECTIVES

What It Is

In Step 6, you check to make sure the tasks on your list will, when completed, produce the objectives you are aiming for. Note in Figure 5.7 that this is symbolic of the interrelatedness of objectives with tasks.

How to Do It

Here is where you may need to be flexible, as we just discussed. As you go through your tasks and objectives, it's essential that the two match up (Figure 5.7). You may find this process of analysis reveals certain anomalies, inconsistencies, or things missing. Let's say you are considering the objective Building Complete. You've gone through your tasks and listed them. But when you go through this

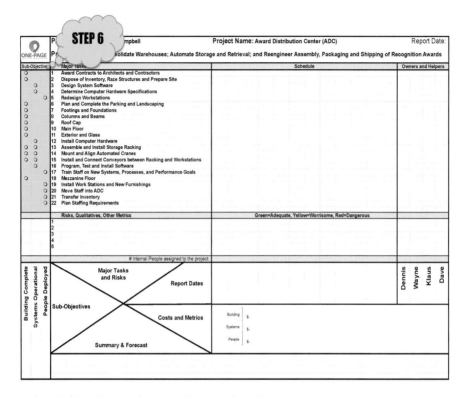

FIGURE 5.7   *Step 6: Aligning Tasks to Sub-Objectives*
Copyright OPPMi 2012. PDF color templates available at www.oppmi.com.

step, aligning the tasks with objectives, you may find you don't have any tasks that relate to completing the building. Go back and add some.

This process of alignment is not something done once and left forever. As you work your way through the project, with each step it is natural to reevaluate succeeding steps. Think of the OPPM as a connective web that supports the entire project. With each step, you have the opportunity to continuously improve.

In fact, I firmly believe one of the greatest strengths of the OPPM is that it has continual improvement embedded in its construction. Don't fight this; instead, use it to your advantage.

However, know that overanalysis is the death of many projects. As I noted before, many of us at O.C. Tanner went to school to study project management, hired consultants, and bought books. At one time, we had 25 forms. Our project management program died under its own weight.

In Figure 5.7 where you see the sub-objectives aligned with major tasks, you can see the process of alignment at work. Award Contracts to Architects and Contractors (Major Task 1) is a task that has to do with the Building Complete objective, and you can see there is a circle where this task and this objective intersect. Awarding contracts has little to do with making the systems operational or deploying people, so there are no circles connecting these objectives to the Award Contracts task.

Design System Software (Major Task 3) and Determine Computer Hardware Specifications (Major Task 4) directly affect the objective of Systems Operational, so they have circles that align them with this sub-objective.

Take a look at the task of Assemble and Install Storage Racking (Major Task 13). It is aligned with two sub-objectives, those of Building Complete and Systems Operational because these 30-foot-high racks are part of the building and also part of the systems we were developing. Train Staff on New Systems, Processes, and Performance Goals (Major Task 17), not surprisingly, is aligned with the People Deployed sub-objective, because the people being deployed in the building have to first be trained.

Some of the tasks are aligned with two objectives, but most are aligned with just one; all tasks are aligned with at least one objective. If a task cannot be aligned to an objective, either there's no point in doing the task and it should not be included in the OPPM, or your sub-objectives are incomplete.

Let me give another quick example of how we aligned particular tasks with an objective. This was with our accounts receivable reduction project. While setting the project up, we realized that in the past, all our energy toward reaching this objective was focused on collections. We tried to get the collections department to be more efficient and effective, thinking it was the heart of the problem.

But as we studied the accounts receivable process, we came to a new realization: the process was more complex and involved more folks than just the collections department. The OPPM forced us to analyze the entire quote-to-cash process, and we ended up dividing it into four sub-processes:

1. *Selling* (selling the product or service)
2. Which leads to the *setup* (recording the sale, setting up the account, doing credit checks, etc.)
3. Which leads to *invoicing* (creating and sending the invoice)
4. Which finally leads to *collecting*

We had been ignoring the first three steps of the process (selling, setup, and invoicing) and putting all our energy into the last step (collecting). But, in fact, all the sets contributed to the problem of us having a large number of accounts receivable at any given time.

Products and services were sold to customers who had unique and diverse payables requirements. Salespeople were paid commissions when awards were shipped and invoiced, not when sales were paid for, so the motivation of the salespeople was quickly diluted following shipment. The program setup process didn't always do a good job at meeting the invoice formatting demands of customers. Customers would want certain formats or information that our invoices did not always provide, and when the formatting wasn't right, they delayed payment. And the invoicing process made mistakes by sending invoices to the wrong person or department or having wrong pricing or other information. No wonder the collections department was having such a hard time collecting!

To use the imagery of Stephen R. Covey, the late author of *The Seven Habits of Highly Effective People*, we were hacking at branches rather than focusing on roots.

To reduce our accounts receivable, we had to improve all our processes. It is this type of insight that can come during the creation of an OPPM.

STEP 7: THE REPORT DATES
What It Is

With this step, shown in Figure 5.8 as a rectangle running left to right near the bottom of the OPPM, we break down

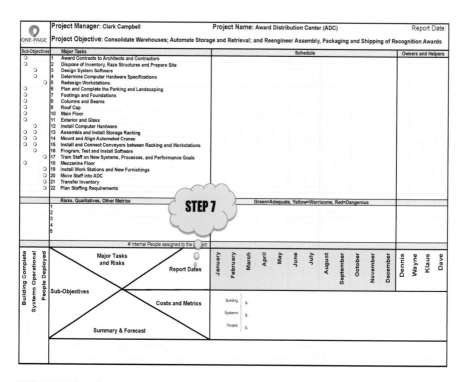

FIGURE 5.8   *Step 7: The Report Dates*

Copyright OPPMi 2012. PDF color templates available at www.oppmi.com.

the timeline into discrete steps, in this case monthly increments. You don't have to break a project down into monthly increments—I've done them every two weeks, once a month, once every two months, and once every three months—but monthly is, from my experience, the most common.

Management determines these dates. We ask management when they want us to report to them, and that's what we format on the OPPM. Also, the length of the reporting periods may vary during a project. For example, as a project is getting off the ground, management may want weekly or biweekly reports, but once the project is under way, monthly reports become adequate.

How to Do It

The first step here is to evaluate the total time horizon for the project. Then, break down the timeline into measurable time buckets—what we referred to earlier when we discussed how to break down a project's time variable.

Before you commit to the timeline, think carefully about what you are committing to. When you let everyone know the project's timeline and time increments, you become responsible for meeting them. As with tasks, you need buy-in from all concerned. You cannot impose a timeline or deadline and expect everyone to jump up and down and say thank you. A timeline is an imposition and obligation, and that's why you need to discuss it with all who will be responsible for meeting it. You need their agreement the timeline is doable and they will perform and meet it.

Eric Verzuh's Chapter 8 on the art and science of estimating provides some tutoring and examples of the tools and techniques available to help you with this and Step 8—your schedule.

STEP 8: ALIGNING TASKS TO REPORT DATES

What It Is

What we are now doing is aligning or connecting the timeline with the tasks—completing the project schedule.

How to Do It

We decide how long each task will take. Then we place an empty circle in the boxes alongside the task. If the task will take seven months and the time buckets are in monthly increments, then there will be seven circles next to this task. As each task is completed, the aligned circle is filled in.

If the scope of a task has expanded since the project's beginning, we use an open square instead of a circle. The reader then knows this task involves more than when the schedule was first established. Like the circles, when a task with a square is completed, this is signified with filling in the square.

Let's look at Figure 5.9, where we have these circles in place. The first task, Award Contracts to Architects and Contractors, has two open circles, in January and February. This means it begins in January, there are two months to complete this task, and it should be finished by the end of February.

 The two open circles do not mean that 50 percent of the work is planned each in January and February. It simply means there is work planned for each of those months. The actual percent planned is not shown on the OPPM and must be retained elsewhere.

Two lines below is Major Task 3, Design System Software. This too starts at the beginning of the project, January, but has four circles. It has four months to be completed. Note

Project Manager: Clark Campbell **Project Name:** Award Distribution Center (ADC) Report Date:

ONE-PAGE **Project Objective:** Consolidate Warehouses; Automate Storage and Retrieval; and Reengineer Assembly, Packaging and Shipping of Recognition Awards

Sub-Objectives	Major Tasks	Schedule	Owners and Helpers
	1 Award Contracts to Architects and Contractors		
	2 Dispose of Inventory, Raze Structures and Prepare Site		
	3 Design System Software		
	4 Determine Computer Hardware Specifications		
	5 Redesign Workstations		
	6 Plan and Complete the Parking and Land		
	7 Footings and Foundations	**STEP 8**	
	8 Columns and Beams		
	9 Roof Cap		
	10 Main Floor		
	11 Exterior and Glass		
	12 Install Computer Hardware		
	13 Assemble and Install Storage Racking		
	14 Mount and Align Automated Cranes		
	15 Install and Connect Conveyors between Racking and Workstations		
	16 Program, Test and Install Software		
	17 Train Staff on New Systems, Processes, and Performance Goals		
	18 Mezzanine Floor		
	19 Install Work Stations and New Furnishings		
	20 Move Staff into ADC		
	21 Transfer Inventory		
	22 Plan Staffing Requirements		

Risks, Qualitatives, Other Metrics	Green=Adequate, Yellow=Worrisome, Red=Dangerous
1	
2	
3	
4	
5	

Internal People assigned to the project: 16 18 16 16 17 16 16 16 18 18 18 18

Building Complete / Systems Operational / People Deployed	Major Tasks and Risks — Report Dates	January	February	March	April	May	June	July	August	September	October	November	December	Dennis	Wayne	Klaus	Dave
Sub-Objectives	Costs and Metrics	Building $-															
		Systems $-															
	Summary & Forecast	People $-															

FIGURE 5.9 *Step 8: Aligning Tasks to Report Dates — The Schedule*
Copyright OPPMi 2012. PDF color templates available at www.oppmi.com.

that the last circle is enclosed in a bold rectangle. These are used to highlight a project's major milestones. This OPPM has four such rectangles. In addition to Design System Software, which is to be completed in April, other major tasks with milestones are Mount and Align Automated Cranes (Major Task 14), whose completion date is August; Train Staff on New Systems, Processes, and Performance Goals (Major Task 17), which has a December completion date; and Transfer Inventory (Major Task 21), showing that we are then able to begin to transfer inventory. Tasks with bold rectangles are key indicators of project performance.

Consider the task on line 6, Plan and Complete the Parking and Landscaping. That has five months for completion, and the first circle is placed in the May column. This means we don't expect this task to start until May, which makes sense because we would expect to complete other tasks first, such as the Footings and Foundations and the Design System Software.

Look at the last task listed, Plan Staffing Requirements, on line 22. Note how interrupted this is in terms of the circles aligned with it. There's a circle in February, and the next one is May, and then there are three starting in September but none in December. That's because staffing isn't done on a regular basis but on an irregular basis, as needed. Train Staff, another task (17), doesn't get started until late in the project, namely September. That's logical because there's no need to start training people to work the building's equipment and systems until the completion of the building is near.

The line asking for number of internal people is also part of Step 8. Internal people are full-time employees of the company and not consultants, sub-contractors, contract workers, or part-timers. It is simply a nose count—the number of employees involved with the project—and does not segregate among internal employees working on the project full time, half time, or some other part of the time.

This is important because project managers must be concerned with resource allocation. The project management office will add up the number of employees involved with each project at the corporation, and this number provides a sense of the organization's commitment to a project. If one project has a nose count of 15 and another has 3, it says a lot about the commitment and resources devoted to each of these projects. This is not a hard number, but it provides the reader with an idea of how many people are involved with the project, which, in turns, allows this project to be compared with other projects.

STEP 9: ALIGNING TASKS AND SCHEDULE TO OWNERS

What It Is

Note that in Figure 5.10, the highlighted areas call out previously completed steps. Attention is drawn to the top right section of the form. With this step, we align tasks to their owners and helpers and assign priorities among them when a task has an owner and helper.

How to Do It

Tasks have owners. Many tasks have more than one owner. There is almost always one main owner, however. The letter A on the OPPM designates that owner. If there is a sub-owner, which I call a helper, a B designates that person, whereas a third owner gets a C. But, let me emphasize again, you should almost never have more than one principal owner for each task. Each task must have someone on the team who has ultimate responsibility. That's why I highlight the principal owners with a blue rectangle: it makes it possible for readers of this OPPM

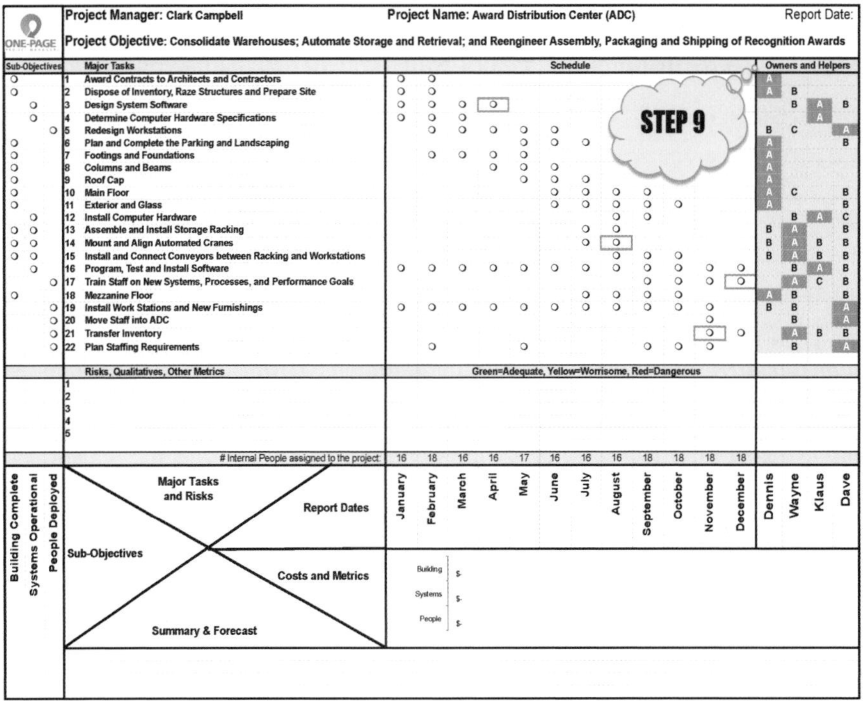

FIGURE 5.10   *Step 9: Aligning Tasks and Schedule to Owners*
Copyright OPPMi 2012. PDF color templates available at www.oppmi.com.

to know immediately who is the principal owner for each task.

If an owner has primary responsibility for such-and-such task, where the row and column for that task and owner intersect, there will be an A. If another owner has secondary responsibility, that person will get a B where his or her column and the task's row intersect. And for a third owner, a C is placed in the same way. You can see these in Figure 5.10 where the Owners and Helpers section is filled in.

Some tasks have only one owner, so the row for that task will have only one letter in this section and that letter will, of course, be an A.

In our filled-in example, you'll see that the first task (line 1), Award Contracts to Architects and Contractors, has one owner, Dennis. With one owner, he gets an A in the box for that task. The third task (line 3), Design System Software, has three owners: Klaus is the A owner and Wayne and Dave are B owners. This means that Klaus is ultimately responsible, and Wayne and Dave have lesser, shared responsibilities for the success of the task. You can have more than one B or C owners, but you should strongly avoid having more than one A owner. Main Floor (line 10) has three owners: Dennis has top priority as indicated by his A; Dave, with his B, has secondary responsibility; and Wayne has tertiary responsibility, which is why he gets a C. Klaus is not involved and therefore gets no letter connected to this task.

Who owns what is decided through a process of collaboration and negotiation with members of the team, with you providing leadership and, if need be, mediation. At the end of this step, personal responsibility is clearly shown along with expectation for assistance.

The process of determining ownership is an exercise in team building, and effective project managers use the OPPM in this way. If you have a team in which a member avoids ownership of the various tasks, this step helps remedy this situation often in a collegial way. Ideally, when going through the project's tasks and looking for owners, you will have team members weighing in, holding up their hands, and volunteering to take on responsibility. When they see that one member perhaps has more A ownership tasks than others, the others might volunteer to be B owners on those tasks and pledge to help out. This is, of course, the ideal.

The reality might be different. You might have a team whose members do little to help one another and who look to do as little as possible. This exercise is a good diagnostic for understanding the strengths of your team and whether you need to use your team-building skills to strengthen the team.

As the project manager, you need to encourage communication between all levels. Yes, I keep coming back to communication, but that's because it is the most essential ingredient for the success of any project. It's okay for a subordinate to go over your head and talk to your superior if that team member feels the need to communicate directly with the superior. What you want is open dialogue. You want your people to feel free to communicate both good and bad news. The OPPM helps foster an environment where communication is encouraged among all involved parties. It opens the door and invites people into your project. A successful project is not managed in a closed office, but only in an open one.

 A key to the success of any project is transparency of communication. Communication must be open, devoid of agendas, and viewable by all constituents.

STEP 10: RISKS, QUALITATIVES, AND OTHER METRICS

What It Is

This is the portion of the OPPM that deals with subjective or qualitative tasks. There are parts of every project that do not easily lend themselves to quantitative analysis on a timeline. You'll find this section open across the entire middle of the page (Figure 5.11).

Software performance is often in this category. We had an enterprise resource planning (ERP) project we

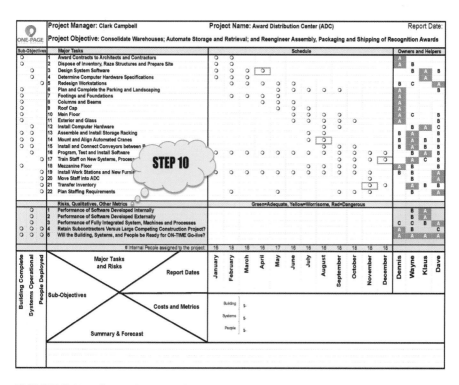

FIGURE 5.11   *Step 10: Risks, Qualitatives, and Other Metrics*

Copyright OPPMi 2012. PDF color templates available at www.oppmi.com.

called Cornerstone. Part of that project involved billing screens that would come up on workers' computers. It wasn't easy to say whether the time it took for the billing screen to come up was adequate or inadequate. This was a judgment call. We could have said that if the screen took more than 2 seconds to come up, the performance was inadequate. But the truth was, we preferred the screen to come up within 0.5 seconds. However, 1 or even 2 seconds was acceptable, if such a slow performance was infrequent.

What about cell phone reception? It might be unacceptable to have a cell phone call be disconnected, but what about when a call has static or otherwise has a connection where it is hard to hear the other caller? When is cell phone reception acceptable, and when is it unacceptable? Situations like these are subjective and hard to objectively quantify.

Not everything in life—or in projects—is a yes or no. This section of the OPPM recognizes this and uses stoplight colors to depict it. We will discuss this in the next chapter.

How to Do It

In Figure 5.11, where the risks and other sub-objectives are filled in, you will find five opportunities for judgment listed: Performance of Software Developed Internally; Performance of Software Developed Externally; Performance of Fully Integrated System, Machines and

Processes; Retain Subcontractors Versus Large Competing Construction Project?; and Will the Building, Systems, and People be Ready for ON-TIME Go-live?

The first three of these all are related to software, and, as we just discussed, it's often hard to quantify how well software performs. Yet, of course, software can be vital (which it certainly was with our ADC); you can't ignore it. It is listed in the OPPM because through site visits with other companies, we were told this was a major risk area for successful deployments of ASRS equipment. The entry Retain Subcontractors Versus Large Competing Construction Project refers to our having to compete for subcontractors with another major construction project going on in the area. The last subjective task, Will the Building, Systems, and People be Ready for ON-TIME Go-live, refers to the project team's best judgment about getting the entire building and its systems operating and doing so according to the project's timeline. Because this is the number one priority for the boss, all owners are A (principal) owners for this task.

Be aware that objectives and owners are aligned with these subjective tasks just as they are with tasks that are more quantifiable. These tasks must be tied to the project's sub-objectives and each must have at least one owner. You'll note that we broke our own rule of only one A owner per task. The OPPM is for projects—not the other way around. It should accommodate your project—your project shouldn't accommodate the OPPM.

STEP 11: COSTS AND METRICS

What It Is

In Figure 5.12 the rectangle in the lower right-hand side of the OPPM is highlighted. This is where the budget is represented. The budget is dealt with in a simple, straightforward manner via bar graphs.

We've divided the budget into three parts: Building ($6.0 million), Systems ($3.0 million), and People ($0.5 million). These are simple bar graphs, and the length of each represents the amount of money for that part of the budget. Although the target dates are listed just above the

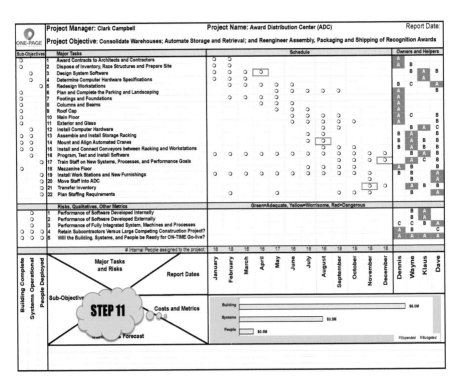

FIGURE 5.12   *Step 11: Costs and Metrics*

budget lines, there is no relation between them. In fact, the budget area stands alone; it is not related to the timeline, the objectives, or the owners. The purpose of this budget graph is to give management a quick, easy-to-understand picture of where the budget is at any given time.

How to Do It

This is very simple—just create bar graphs for each portion of the budget. Use green to show when the project is on budget, yellow when it is running over budget but recoverable, and red to show it is incurably over budget. It is vital that as you draw up the budget bars, you work closely with the accounting department so you use accurate information.

Showing the budget on the OPPM is easy; deriving it is much more difficult. Before you draw up the budget, be sure you know all your costs. For example, when drawing up the budget for ADC, before we established the budget, we had agreements with our suppliers about what they would do, when, and for how much. Only when we had a clear and complete picture of costs were we willing to commit to a budget. Be sure you include all costs—software licenses, software support contracts, consultants, travel, training, and the like. Include provisions for incremental increases, such as those resulting from inflation or changes in the project. Depending on how your organization operates, you may include in the budget "soft costs," such as internal people from your company who spend some or all of their time on your project. We did not report these costs on the OPPM.

You will also see that the three budget bars add to $9.5 million. We secured $10.0 million, which included $500,000 for unplanned contingencies. Some put a contingency bar in this section and track those expenses too.

STEP 12: SUMMARY & FORECAST

What It Is

You have now completed all of your OPPM except for the small Summary & Forecast section along the bottom of the page (Figure 5.13). With the first edition of your OPPM, at

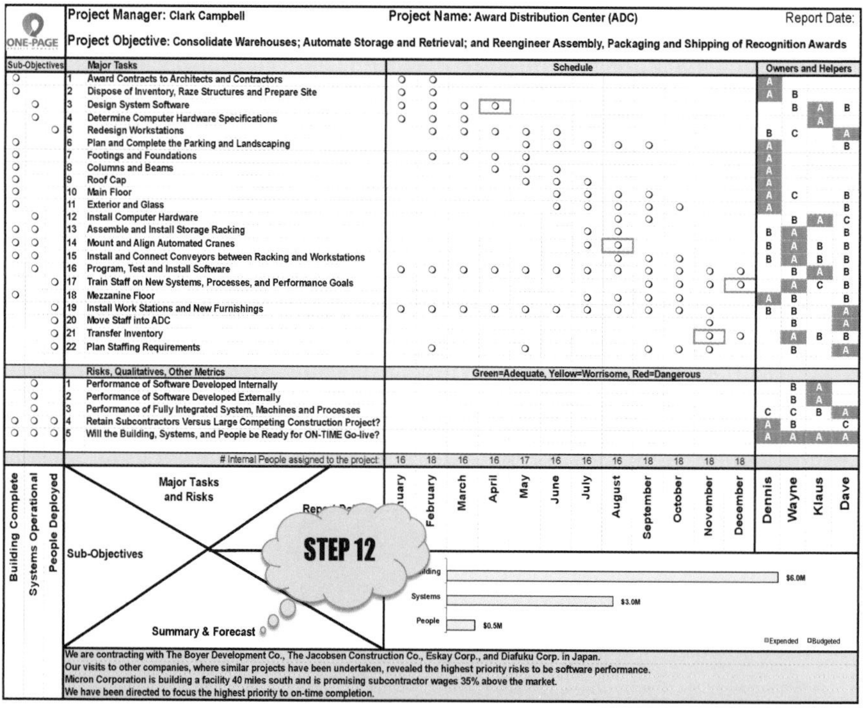

FIGURE 5.13   *Step 12: The Summary and Forecast*

Copyright OPPMi 2012. PDF color templates available at www.oppmi.com.

the start of the project, this section is where you add the finishing touches to your plan. A good summary at this point clears up any ambiguities or glaring questions and heads off potential future misunderstandings. Everybody should now be "reading from the same page"—both literally and metaphorically. It is here where you are committing yourself, saying this is your final plan.

Furthermore, it is this completed edition of the OPPM that is used to get final approval for your plan from upper management. It is the means by which you let management know the project's objectives, tasks, owners, budget, and timeline. It is easy to see that after management approves your project with the completed OPPM, there is an easily communicated yet comprehensive meeting of the minds.

In subsequent OPPMs, you use the Summary & Forecast section to write down information about how the project is doing. It communicates the project status at any given time and what you forecast for the immediate future. Here, you write as succinctly and comprehensively as possible.

How to Do It

The amount of space available for the summary is limited—on purpose. Limiting the space forces you to be selective about what you are describing and efficient in your discussion. Upper-level management isn't going to read lengthy treatises about different aspects of the project. Senior managers want to know what's going on and to learn that as quickly as possible (Figure 5.13).

 Explain everything needed in the Summary & Forecast space. Do not attach additional pages or diagrams; management won't read them. This is a one-page project manager, which means everything must be contained on this single piece of 8 1/2-inch-by-11-inch paper. This tool, when compiled correctly, stands on its own.

The Summary & Forecast section is important. It is where you communicate to your readers information that is not obvious or contained in the rest of the OPPM. Here you answer the obvious, unanswered questions exposed by the completed information on the OPPM. For example, if the project were over budget, that would be discussed here. If there are holdups because of problems with suppliers, causing various aspects of the project to fall behind schedule, here's your chance to let your readers know why things are late.

This is your opportunity to make things clear, to set things straight, and to avoid misinterpretation. But don't tell management what is obvious. Don't say, "The System expenses are running over budget," or "Exterior and glass is running late." Such information, although true, is also obvious to anyone reading the OPPM.

TiP The Summary & Forecast should be about why, what you are going to do about it, and what you expect to happen.

The Summary & Forecast should focus on the whys that the OPPM reveal: why you are behind schedule, why you are over budget, why there are cost overruns, why this circle isn't filled in as it should be, and why that line is red instead of green.

After you explain the why, you explain what you are going to do about it and then you forecast what will happen.

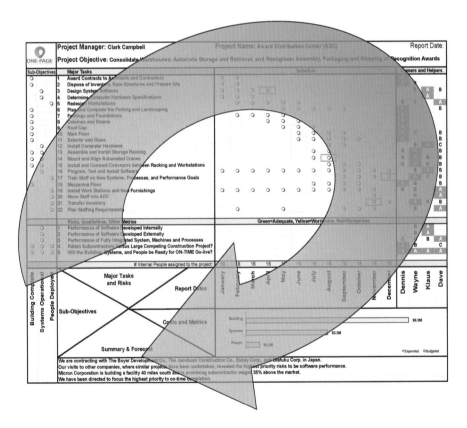

FIGURE 5.14   *Reading the OPPM*

Copyright OPPMi 2012. PDF color templates available at www.oppmi.com.

The Summary & Forecast section is where you explain to management those things that cannot be conveyed with any of the various integrated sections of the OPPM.

THE 12 STEPS COME TOGETHER

OPPMs are read clockwise, as shown in Figure 5.14. You begin at the left with the sub-objectives and proceed around to tasks, schedule, owners, costs, and finally the summary and a forecast of what's next for the project.

The Five Reporting Steps for a Traditional OPPM, or OPPM in Action

Before showing how the one-page project manager (OPPM) was used during the year our Award Distribution Center (ADC) project took, I think it worthwhile for you to review the version we developed before the project began (see Figure 4.4). This was a very important document and the most referenced page in the final funding proposal and approval to launch. It was the opening slide and closing slide in the approval presentation and was the only piece of paper many wanted to retain. **It communicated the project plan.**

Now, years later, the OPPM is a simple attachment to an e-mail.

FIVE STEPS TO CREATING A REPORT USING THE OPPM

We are now ready to use our freshly built OPPM. The careful work and team building required to construct your OPPM now pays off. Monthly reports are easy when you follow the five steps in Figure 6.1.

You meet with your project's owners near the conclusion of each report date and complete the following tasks:

1. Bold the report date.
2. Fill in major tasks' progress. Designate the project's progress by filling in the dots. Although filling in the

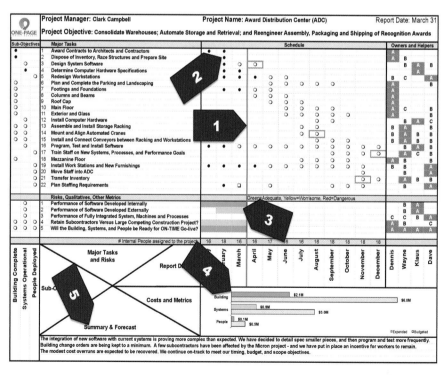

FIGURE 6.1   *The Five Traditional Reporting Steps*

Copyright OPPMi 2012. PDF color templates available at www.oppmi.com.

dots is easy, getting agreement on which to fill in, or not fill in, is often anything but easy. Some team members will say, "Yes, fill in my dot," and others may say, "That's not done yet."

CONCEPT A filled-in dot means that the worked planned for that period is complete.

Your job as project manager is to bring the team together. This requires straight talk—very direct, unambiguous communication. Once you decide which dots to fill in and which not to, the team must agree. When the OPPM is completed, you can't have a team member say that the report is not quite accurate or is not candid—or that the team is being anything less than honest. If this happens, the efficacy and credibility of the OPPM is undermined. The project team absolutely must be unified, and the team leader must work with team members until they agree. Only then should the OPPM be signed and submitted to upper management.

3. Designate qualitative performance in the Risks, Qualitatives, Other Metrics section. Use stoplight colors when designating qualitative performance. Before you start the project, clearly define what each color means. The project leader does this in conjunction with team members. You and your team may have your own definitions of the colors, and they may vary a bit from project to project. Here is how many organizations define them:

- **Green: Adequate performance**—Performance is good enough, but not perfect or without a minor issue or two. Much is known about the time and high cost of perusing that last requirement to reach near perfection. A word of caution: this stretching for the flawless is valued differently for every project. Consider our Boeing 737 project—adequate is indeed near-perfection. Consider our ADC project—adequate is "good enough for now."
- **Yellow: Worrisome performance**—Performance may affect the timing, scope, or cost of the project. Problems designated with yellow are expected to be transient and solvable by the team without outside help.
- **Red: Dangerous performance**—Performance will affect the timing, scope, or budget of the project. To resolve these tasks, efforts beyond those of the individual task owner, or the project team, will be required. Red may also mean the issue cannot be fixed.

4. Report expenditures. Figures should come from the accounting department, which must be in agreement with how the budget is portrayed on the OPPM. Actual expenditures are shown as a bar juxtaposed to the budget. This gives a clear picture of the amount of the budget spent to date and whether you are spending above, under, or on budget. Again, colors are used:

- **Green:** Project is on or under budget.
- **Yellow:** Project is over budget, but you either expect to find savings to eventually return to budget or are within a previously agreed to contingency percentage (some use less than 10 percent over).
- **Red:** Project is over budget, and you expect to end the project over budget and over any previously approved contingency percentage.

5. Complete the Summary & Forecast section. Be succinct. Do not explain that which the OPPM displays. Answer the questions posed by empty circles and colors other than green. Conclude with what's next.

EXAMPLES OF THE OPPM IN ACTION

The red vertical line is where we are today. The circles show where each task is on the timeline.

Figures 6.2, 6.3, and 6.4 show how the OPPM changes over time as a project progresses. The ADC project began in January and ended in December, one year later. We will examine the OPPM reports for March, July, and November.

The OPPM should be completed in a timely manner. If it is weeks late, it is not as useful. If the time allotments used are monthly, then the tool should be completed within five working days of the end of each month. This work is not onerous when an OPPM is in place. Our surveys indicate that most users are able to complete a report in less than 19 minutes.

When completing the OPPM, you and your team (the owners) craft a first draft, then open up the discussion to the others involved with the project. Ask if they think the OPPM you and your team have created accurately represents where the project is currently. This helps engage a wide group of interested parties, it brings in new ideas, and—very important—it helps maintain the honesty and integrity of the owners. When owners collaborate with other stakeholders, they become more likely to be accurate and realistic with their claims. They may want to say a certain task is on time, for example, but following some serious outreach, they may change their minds and find the task is somewhat behind schedule.

 Broad collaboration is practical only because **CONCEPT** OPPMs contain a limited number of circles. This is a valuable demonstration of "serious simplicity."

A REPORT EARLY IN THE PROJECT

The vertical red line tells you where you are in the life span of the project. Figure 6.2 is the March report; therefore, the red line is right of the March target date. The upper right-hand corner also specifies the date, so the reader can quickly see the time period the OPPM is referring to.

Note the black dots. The first two tasks (on the OPPM we call them Major Tasks, but for efficiency, we will call them "tasks" going forward), Award Contracts to Architects and Contractors (line 1) and Dispose of Inventory, Raze Structures and Prepare Site (line 2), were supposed to

Project Manager: Clark Campbell **Project Name:** Award Distribution Center (ADC) **Report Date:** March 31

ONE-PAGE

Project Objective: Consolidate Warehouses; Automate Storage and Retrieval; and Reengineer Assembly, Packaging and Shipping of Recognition Awards

Sub-Objectives	Major Tasks		Owners and Helpers
	1	Award Contracts to Architects and Contractors	A
	2	Dispose of Inventory, Raze Structures and Prepare Site	A B
	3	Design System Software	B A B
	4	Determine Computer Hardware Specifications	A
	5	Redesign Workstations	B C A
	6	Plan and Complete the Parking and Landscaping	A B
	7	Footings and Foundations	A
	8	Columns and Beams	A
	9	Roof Cap	A
	10	Main Floor	A C B
	11	Exterior and Glass	A B
	12	Install Computer Hardware	B A C
	13	Assemble and Install Storage Racking	B A B
	14	Mount and Align Automated Cranes	B A B
	15	Install and Connect Conveyors between Racking and Workstations	B A B B
	16	Program, Test and Install Software	B A B
	17	Train Staff on New Systems, Processes, and Performance Goals	A C B
	18	Mezzanine Floor	B
	19	Install Work Stations and New Furnishings	B B A
	20	Move Staff into ADC	B A
	21	Transfer Inventory	A B B
	22	Plan Staffing Requirements	B A

Schedule: January, February, March, April, May, June, July, August, September, October, November, December

Risks, Qualitatives, Other Metrics		
1	Performance of Software Developed Internally	B A
2	Performance of Software Developed Externally	B A
3	Performance of Fully Integrated System, Machines and Processes	C B A
4	Retain Subcontractors Versus Large Competing Construction Project?	A B C
5	Will the Building, Systems, and People be Ready for ON-TIME Go-live?	A A A A

Green=Adequate, Yellow=Worrisome, Red=Dangerous

Internal People assigned to the project: 16 18 16 16 17 16 16 16 18 18 18 18

Building Complete / Systems Operational / People Deployed

Major Tasks and Risks — Report Dates

Sub-Objectives

Costs and Metrics

Summary & Forecast

Owners and Helpers: Dennis, Wayne, Klaus, Dave

Costs and Metrics:
- Building: $2.1M Expended / $6.0M Budgeted
- Systems: $0.9M Expended / $3.0M Budgeted
- People: $0.1M Expended / $0.5M Budgeted

The integration of new software with current systems is proving more complex than expected. We have decided to detail spec smaller pieces, and then program and test more frequently. Building change orders are being kept to a minimum. A few subcontractors have been affected by the Micron project - and we have put in place an incentive for workers to remain. The modest cost overruns are expected to be recovered. We continue on-track to meet our timing, budget, and scope objectives.

FIGURE 6.2 *The ADC March Report*

be completed within the first two months of the project. Looking at Figure 6.2, you don't know when they were completed, but you know they are finished at this time; the previous OPPM, for February, would have told you if the tasks were completed exactly on time. The third task, Design System Software (line 3), is behind schedule (there is an empty circle in March). Also, it is clear that the April major milestone is in jeopardy. The fourth task, Determine Computer Hardware Specifications (line 4), is on time because all the dots up to the present are black. The next task, Redesign Workstations (line 5), is ahead of schedule (there is a black circle to the right of the red line in the April column). Notice how easily and quickly a reader can ascertain which tasks are on time, ahead of schedule or behind, and are currently completed.

When you look at Risks, Qualitatives, Other Metrics (lines 1 through 5), you will see filled-in boxes extending to the right. In the March illustration, Performance of Software Developed Internally (line 1) and Will the Building, Systems, and People be Ready for ON-TIME Go-live (line 5) both have green boxes for each month of the project up to the present (March). The green says internal software is performing adequately and we are confident of an on-time go-live. Performance of Software Developed Externally (line 2) has yellow boxes beginning in the second month (February) and continuing into March. This means work began in February and, because the boxes are yellow, performance is worrisome. Performance of Fully Integrated System, Machines and Processes (line 3) doesn't have filled boxes (line 3) because no work has begun. A series of yellow boxes on line 5 shows we continue to worry about subcontractors being enticed away.

The OPPM also links tasks to sub-objectives. Notice that the first two tasks, Award Contracts to Architects and Contractors (line 1) and Dispose of Inventory, Raze Structures and Prepare Site (line 2), have every circle on the timeline filled in, indicating they are finished. Therefore, the sub-objectives connected to these tasks (Building Complete) also have black circles. As you look ahead to Figures 6.3

and 6.4, you see that as tasks are completed, progress in meeting the project sub-objectives is visible.

The mechanism for this is quite simple. As a task is completed, the circle(s) aligned with the sub-objective(s) is filled in.

Budget and Costs

The bars near the bottom of the page show cost performance. Each category of the budget—Building, Systems, and People—has two bars. The bottom is in gray and reminds the reader how much has been budgeted for that category. Six million dollars has been budgeted for the building, $3 million for systems, and $500,000 for people. The running bars above each gray bar show how much has actually been spent on each segment of the budget at the time of the report. A green bar means that segment is currently on plan or below, a yellow bar indicates we are worried (usually means more than 10 percent over) the segment is in danger of going over budget, and a red line states clearly the segment is dangerously over budget and is likely to remain so.

The building budget is a green bar at $2.1 million. This means that at the end of March, $2.1 million of the $6.0 million total building budget has been spent and that these expenditures are proceeding as or better than planned. Of the system's $3.0 million budget, $0.9 has been spent. This bar is yellow, which tells management this portion of the project is over budget but recoverable. The people portion is relatively small and is on plan at around $100,000.

Summary & Forecast

In this section we don't reexplain what is revealed via display, and we strive to answer questions raised by late open circles, yellows, and reds. We also want to comment on what's next and provide a little look into the future. We read, "The integration of new software with current systems is proving more complex than expected" [the why for the open circles and first yellow boxes]. "We have decided to detail spec smaller pieces, and then program and test more frequently" [what's next]. "A few subcontractors have been affected by the Micron project—and we have put in place an incentive for workers to remain" [the why for yellows on risk line 4 and the additional scope to develop a mitigating plan represented by the open square on line 22]. "The modest cost overruns are expected to be recovered" [comment on the yellow systems bar].

A REPORT MIDWAY THROUGH THE PROJECT

Again, the essence of the OPPM is comprehended quickly by reading in a circle (see Figure 5.14)—from Sub-Objectives to Major Tasks and Risks to Schedule to Owners and Helpers to Costs and Metrics to Summary & Forecast. The illustration for July (see Figure 6.3) shows more dots filled in, which is what you would expect as a project progresses. Notice how many tasks are now behind schedule. Plan and Complete the Parking and Landscaping (line 6) has two empty circles and is therefore two months behind. The comment in the Summary &

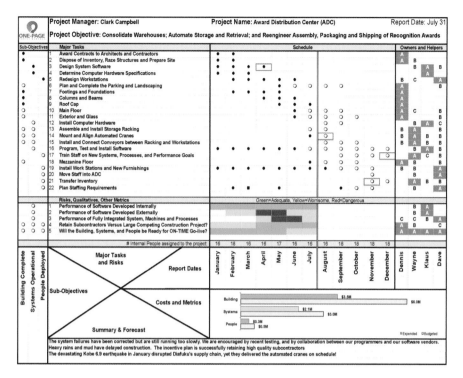

Project Manager: Clark Campbell		Project Name: Award Distribution Center (ADC)		Report Date: July 31

Project Objective: Consolidate Warehouses; Automate Storage and Retrieval; and Reengineer Assembly, Packaging and Shipping of Recognition Awards

FIGURE 6.3   *The ADC July Report*

Copyright OPPMi 2012. PDF color templates available at www.oppmi.com.

Forecast at the bottom of the page explains this lateness: "Heavy rains and mud have delayed construction" [the why]. "Plans are in place to catch up" [what you are doing about it and what you expect will happen]. Other late tasks include Main Floor (line 10); Exterior and Glass (line 11); Assemble and Install Storage Racking (line 13); Mount and Align Automated Cranes (line 14); and Program, Test and Install Software (line 16).

You don't want to sugarcoat or gloss over potential problems. You want to be honest and forthright but still positive. The Summary states: "Meeting our go-live objective of Dec. 31 remains in jeopardy but we are more optimistic than last month." This is an honest assessment of the situation. The project was in jeopardy of not being completed on time, but the situation had improved enough that the project team was feeling more optimistic about meeting the ultimate deadline (in fact, it was met).

Tasks now completed include Award Contracts to Architects and Contractors (line 1); Dispose of Inventory, Raze Structures and Prepare Site (line 2); Design System Software (line 3); Determine Computer Hardware Specifications (line 4); and Redesign Workstations (line 5). Also completed are Footings and Foundations (line 7), Columns and Beams (line 8), and Roof Cap (line 9).

Other tasks have not yet begun. You can tell when they are due to start by the month in which the first circle is located. For example, Install Computer Hardware (line 12) will start in August; Train Staff on New Systems, Processes, and Performance Goals (line 17) will start in September; Move Staff into ADC (line 20) begins and ends in November; and Transfer Inventory (line 21) starts in November and is planned to take two months.

Under Risks, Qualitatives, Other Metrics, Figure 6.4 indicates that Performance of Software Developed Internally (line 1) has been adequately operating for the entire project. Will the Building, Systems, and People be Ready for ON-TIME Go-live? (line 5) was, for the first five months, green, but circumstances have put the project's final deadline in jeopardy and that's why it's had yellow for the past two months. Both Performance of Software

Developed Externally (line 2) and Performance of Fully Integrated System, Machines and Processes (line 3) are now yellow, meaning they are having recoverable performance issues. Previously, they each had two months of red, which meant those tasks were so dysfunctional that they jeopardized the entire project.

Budget and Costs

Since Figure 6.2, the building budget graph has moved right, indicating $3.5 million has been spent. It still is green, which says all is well. A total of $2.1 million has been spent on systems, and it remains yellow and worrisome. The people budget has been more than 50 percent consumed (the line is more than halfway filled in), and because the line is green, it remains on budget.

The Summary & Forecast section addresses explanations for late tasks, system challenges, and budget overruns, while giving a studied look into the near future. Some optimism is reflected in both the language and the graphics, especially given the two previous month's reports.

One of the unintended yet valuable consequences of the OPPM became apparent to us about halfway through the ADC project. We held a project team meeting every week in a high-rise building adjacent to and overlooking the ADC. The OPPM became an integral part of those meetings because we all knew we would need to send it to management at the end of the month.

Our meetings improved. We reasoned that using the OPPM provides numerous benefits, including:

- Every project meeting, from general management to project team meetings, is shorter, more efficient, and more effective.
- The agenda for each meeting relating to each project always contains one common element—the project's OPPM.
- Each participant becomes very familiar with the OPPM and how it works because it is used ubiquitously within the organization.
- Everyone at every meeting knows what will be discussed and what he or she will need to report on and can therefore come prepared.
- Less time is spent at meetings and more time is spent running the project.
- Communication to all interested parties is simple—they can each get a copy of the OPPM. You can't readily send Microsoft Project or Primavera (project management software products) to the board of directors or other stakeholders, but you can send the OPPM to all of them.
- The simplicity and directness of the OPPM drives efficiency and straight talk.

A REPORT NEAR THE END OF THE PROJECT

In Figure 6.4, all the tasks but three were due to be completed. Two of these three were completed early—Train

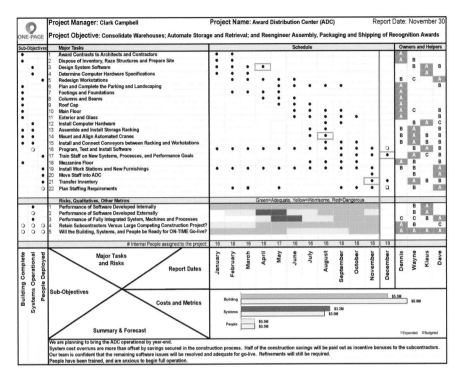

FIGURE 6.4   *The ADC November Report*

Copyright OPPMi 2012. PDF color templates available at www.oppmi.com.

Staff on New Systems, Processes, and Performance Goals
(line 17) and Transfer Inventory (line 21) — and Program,
Test and Install Software (line 16) is on schedule and
planned for completion next month.

Four of our five risk-focused judgment calls are working
well (those in green), but performance of externally developed software demonstrated worrisome issues again in
November after three months of adequate operations.
Look closely at the sub-objectives aligned with our risks.
Two — Performance of Software Developed Internally
(line 1) and Performance of Fully Integrated System,

Machines and Processes (line 3)—have circles for their sub-objectives filled in, indicating the deliverables associated with these tasks are complete. But the other three tasks still have sub-objectives left to wrap up. Retain Subcontractors Versus Large Competing Construction Project? (line 4) and Will the Building, Systems, and People be Ready for ON-TIME Go-live? (line 5) have green boxes. It is important to note the one remaining risk, Performance of Software Developed Externally (line 2), has a yellow line and still shows symptoms of sluggish performance but is not poor enough to cause a recommendation to delay go-live.

Budget and Costs

The building has used $5.3 million of the $6.0 allotted; it is under budget and green. Systems are red. For months we have reported yellow, but now, irreversibly over the total budget, we must report a red. You can see how much over budget the system costs are by looking at the $3.2 million figure in the bar graph and the $3.0 million allocated to this in the budget. With still a month left to the project, the system portion of the project is $200,000 over budget. The people budget is still green and has nearly filled its bar graph, showing that almost all of the $500,000 allocated to people has been spent.

Summary & Forecast

The Summary begins, "We are planning to bring the ADC operational by year-end." We were adequately confident in meeting this highest-priority deliverable. The Summary also addresses cost, which was the next highest priority: "System cost overruns are more than offset by savings secured in the construction process." This tells management that now, near the very end of the project, savings in the construction side of the project will offset the cost overruns that have been seen for months with the system. The software systems issues are much improved and now "adequate for go-live." However, "refinements will still be required" following start-up. You will see a new open square on line 22. This reflects a newly planned recognition event to acknowledge the performance of the project team, outside vendors, contractors, and programmers.

If we remember back more than a year ago, to Step 1 of the 12 construction steps, we said, "You, as project manager, will be making decisions and giving direction to your project. That often means making trade-offs. As part of completing the header, discuss with the boss your eventual need to make these trade-offs affecting cost, schedule, scope, quality, and risks. You and the boss must share a clear understanding of priorities. On-time completion of the ADC was most important to my boss. Followed closely by cost. We then knew, for example, that when balancing schedule against scope, meeting our deadlines would take precedence."

Now, as we plan to come live at year end (which we did), the value of that early collaboration is clearly manifest in bringing a project to successful conclusion—with success being defined in the beginning by the boss—be on time first, be on budget second, and then deliver scope that is good enough, having successfully mitigated the most challenging risks.

Postscript: Today, as I write this book, a decade and a half later, the ADC continues to provide consolidated warehousing with even faster automated storage and retrieval cranes and reliable computer systems assembling recognition awards of world-class quality delivered to clients when promised better than 99 percent of the time.

An Agile Project

Five Essential Parts of an Agile Project

In this and the next two chapters, we introduce the agile one-page project manager (OPPM). We will be specifically discussing agile not traditional project management; however, the basic presentation is similar to the traditional OPPM we covered in Chapters 4, 5, and 6. There are five essential parts to an agile project, 12 construction steps to creating an agile OPPM, and seven reporting steps.

We will discuss the "seriously simple" fundamental principles and practices of agile with a general focus on agile/Scrum. But agile will be discussed only sufficiently enough to provide the background necessary to present the agile OPPM as a communication tool specifically designed for agile/Scrum projects. The following websites offer more detailed information on the agile method:

- Agile Alliance (www.agilealliance.org): a "nonprofit organization with global membership committed to advancing Agile development principles and practices."

- ScrumAlliance (www.scrumalliance.org): "a not-for-profit professional membership organization created to share Scrum framework and transform the world of work."

- The Project Management Institute (www.pmi.org): "the world's leading not-for-profit membership association for the project management profession."

These organizations, together with thousands of traditional and agile books, plus a plethora of trainers and consultants, provide today's project manager with a remarkable breadth and depth of content and recognized certifications.

The American Heritage Dictionary of the English Language, 4th ed., as used on the Free Dictionary website, defines *agile* as "characterized by quickness, lightness, and ease of movement; nimble." This definition certainly applies to agile project management, which has a nimbleness and quickness not found in traditional project management approaches.

The struggles project managers had while managing software development projects led to agile's creation. It remains primarily a software development practice but is now successfully migrating into other areas. In the software development world, the word *agile* incorporates the adaptive and client collaborative elements of lean principles, Scrum methodology, and extreme programming (XP).

Agile project management is not a mature enough practice where everyone has come to an absolute agreement as to what it is and how to define it. Some practitioners stress the lean aspects of agile, whereas others talk about adaptive programming and others emphasize client involvement and collaboration.

The agile movement itself was a reflection of a revolution of sorts against traditional project management. Issues with the traditional waterfall methods, coupled with a disproportionate number of failing technical projects, accelerated the efforts of academics and practitioners alike to come together and share best practices.

In 2001, 17 technical project management leaders gathered at the Snowbird ski resort in Utah and came away with the Agile Manifesto. As outlined on the website (www.agilemanifesto.org), the statement of values relating to agile methodology was as follows:

- Individuals and interactions take precedent over process and tools.
- Working software takes precedent over comprehensive documentation.
- Customer collaboration takes precedent over contract negotiation.
- Responding to change takes precedent over following a plan.

This group then fashioned 12 agile principles supportive of their vision. These principles illustrate the perfect balance of content versus brevity and of sufficiency and efficiency. So much so that they are included here without elaboration.

1. *Our highest priority is to satisfy the customer through early and continuous delivery of valuable software.*

2. *Welcome changing requirements, even late in development. Agile processes harness change for the customer's competitive advantage.*

3. *Deliver working software frequently, from a couple of weeks to a couple of months, with a preference to the shorter timescale.*

4. *Business people and developers must work together daily throughout the project.*

5. *Build projects around motivated individuals. Give them the environment and support they need, and trust them to get the job done.*

6. *The most efficient and effective method of conveying information to and within a development team is face-to-face conversation.*

7. *Working software is the primary measure of progress.*

8. *Agile processes promote sustainable development. The sponsors, developers, and users should be able to maintain a constant pace indefinitely.*

9. *Continuous attention to technical excellence and good design enhances agility.*

10. *Simplicity—the art of maximizing the amount of work not done—is essential.*

11. *The best architectures, requirements, and designs emerge from self-organizing teams.*

12. *At regular intervals, the team reflects on how to become more effective, then tunes and adjusts its behavior accordingly.*

The tenets of "agility" may be applied to both information technology (IT) and non-IT projects. The fundamentals include:

- The desire and ability to reprioritize and respond to change rapidly
- A collaborative, self-organizing, client-centered team
- Incremental iterative delivery of working solutions

Scrum is the most widely used agile methodology and the one I employ. In case you are wondering, before being applied to project management the word *scrum* was used primarily to refer to a rugby play where players must work together to get the ball. John C. Goodpasture, in his book *Project Management the Agile Way: Making It Work in the Enterprise* (Plantation, FL: J. Ross Publishing, 2010), notes: "The objective [of a rugby scrum] is to move the ball using tactics that are improved and self-directed by team members in real time." It is the teamwork that made the word *scrum* so apropos for agile project management.

In the consulting and training we do, we provide the follow description of Scrum:

- Scrum is an agile process that allows us to focus on delivering the highest business value in the shortest time.

- It allows us to rapidly and repeatedly inspect actual working software (every two weeks to one month).
- It requires the business to set the priorities. Teams self-organize to determine the best way to deliver the highest-priority features.
- Every two weeks to a month, anyone can see real working software and decide to release it as is or continue to enhance it for a future release.

The characteristics of agile/Scrum include:

- Teams that are self-organizing
- Requirements, which are captured and refined as items in continuously updated backlogs
- Product that progresses in a series of sprints and releases
- Specific engineering practices, which are not prescribed
- Generative rules that create an agile environment

To describe agile and Scrum methodology, it is helpful to give an example of it in action. Let's say your organization is developing the software for a global positioning satellite (GPS) device used to help automobile drivers find their way. A series of features will be included in the device, but the client (say, the marketing and upper management folks) need to decide, in collaboration with an agile product owner, which features to include and which are not worth the time and effort to develop and to continually prioritize as the project progresses.

The company may go with a product that is "good enough" or top of the line. For example, the product may display diagrams of maps and roadways that show where to go but not have an audio component that speaks directions to the user. Or perhaps the device will have both visual and audio components. Or perhaps the device will have both visual and audio components but will use only a woman's voice. Or it may be decided to include both a man and a woman's voice and let the user decide which to use. Or a series of voices speaking English may be offered, each with a different accent, such as American, British, French, and Irish.

With software especially, it is possible to create products in iterations. Let's assume the company decides that, to be competitive, all of these features are needed but that fully developing all of them will take so long they will be introduced over time.

Initially, the GPS will be introduced with graphics and a woman's voice, and an update three months later will include a man's voice and three months later, voices using different accents. The company is rolling out these features over time.

Not every project can be developed iteratively, which is why agile methodology is appropriate in some situations but not others. If building an airplane, for example, you could not usefully develop the wings and deliver them by themselves and then follow later with the fuselage then the engines then the cockpit instruments and then the passenger seats. That makes no sense because the customer

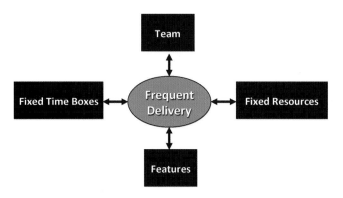

FIGURE 7.1   *The Five Essential Elements of an Agile Project*
Copyright OPPMi 2012.

cannot use the product until it is complete, whereas a GPS with limited features can still be highly useful.

Note that Figure 7.1, which shows the essential elements of an agile project, resembles Figure 4.1, a depiction of traditional methodology. But whereas in the traditional world we focus to a degree on individual owners, in the agile world we think in terms of teams. In the traditional world we manage costs, whereas in the agile world resources are fixed. Time management is essential to the traditionalist, whereas the agile practitioner plans for fixed time boxes. Traditional tasks cascade like a waterfall, completed step by completed step, toward a "big bang" finale. Agile pursues frequent delivery by releasing features in "little bangs."

Let's look at each of these five elements of agile methodology more closely. Figure 7.2 will help because it has a breakdown of each of these elements.

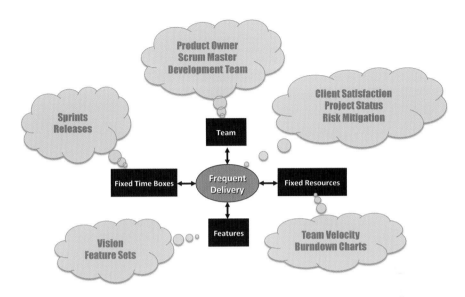

FIGURE 7.2   *Breakdowns of the Agile Five*
Copyright OPPMi 2012.

1. Team:
    Product owner
    - Defines and prioritizes product features for the team
    - Realigns features and priorities every iteration as needed
    - Determines date for releases
    - Accepts or rejects work results

    Scrum Master
    - Coaches collaboration and cooperation
    - Represents management to the team
    - Removes impediments and interference
    - Encourages productivity

Development team
- Self-organizing
- Fixed at five to nine members for each sprint
- Cross-functional (designers, programmers, testers . . .)
- Full time

2. Fixed resources:
- Team velocity—This is the measure of agile team productivity calculated by summing the number of units of work completed in a certain time interval. The units of work may be development hours or agile "story points." Scrum Masters monitor velocity and development teams seek to increase it. Velocity is an important value needed to scope the project initially and to size product and sprint backlogs.
- Burndown charts—These are graphical displays of development work remaining to do versus time. The vertical axis is backlog left to accomplish during the designated time box. The horizontal axis is time, like the 10 working days in a two-week sprint.

    The farthest point to the left, which is also the highest point on the vertical axis, is the total estimated work for the sprint. The farthest point to the right is the predicted end date of the sprint. A straight line plotted between these two points is the expected burndown of the backlog, with its slope being the expected team velocity. As work is completed, the actual remaining backlog is plotted, creating a descending line. Progress-versus-plan is the difference between these two lines. Even knowing all this, many find it counterintuitive to see that above the line is bad and below is good. We seem to be programmed to want up to be better. Nonetheless, the burndown chart is a very powerful tool for the agile project manager to monitor and communicate project status.

3. Features:
   - Vision—An agile vision is a project objective with a "yeah-but." It is a definition of customer-centered business goals the project is intended to accomplish, acknowledging yeah-but they might change.
   - Feature sets—Following the lead from XP, the agile community has adopted the term *feature* from the idea of feature-driven development (FDD). A feature is a small, client-valued function. Feature sets are simply related features organized into sets.

4. Fixed time boxes:
   - Sprints—Sprints are typically a two- to four-week period in agile/Scrum wherein the development team incrementally creates one or more potentially shippable product increments. Features planned for the sprint are drawn from the product backlog, which is a prioritized group of high-level development requirements.
   - Releases—A release is a planning and delivery cycle and may result from one or more sprints. Alan Shalloway, in the essay, *Stellar Performer: The Agile Approach to Software Development,* which appeared in *The Fast Forward MBA in*

Project Management, 4th ed., by Eric Verzuh (Hoboken, NJ: John Wiley & Sons, 2012), discusses the notion of a minimal marketable feature (MMF). "An MMF is a feature that is as small as possible while still providing value and being worth the transaction cost of delivery. Thinking in terms of MMFs is what makes incremental delivery possible. It does require the business to think in a new way: how to split up the overall functionality so as to deliver the greatest value over time."

5. Frequent delivery:

- Client satisfaction—This is the first principle of agile: "Our highest priority is to satisfy the customer through early and continuous delivery of valuable software." Chris Mann, of the University of Calgary, posted a paper on the Internet that followed a two-year industrial study. It was titled "A Case Study on the Impact of Scum on Overtime and Customer Satisfaction," and it concludes: "After Scrum was introduced the customer satisfaction increased while at the same time overtime for the developers decreased (allowing the developers to work at a sustainable pace)." Also, the third agile principle, "Deliver working software frequently," is customer satisfying.

- Project status—Communicating project performance compared with the project plan is the status. Traditional project management gives strong attention to cost and schedule status. The status of agile projects, with fixed time boxes and fixed resources, is more concentrated on frequent delivery of working solutions. The agile burnup chart is a visual display of completed work. Agile status is best observed by going in person to the agile team room where the various components of status emanate from the charts, graphs, backlogs, and displays referred to as information radiators hanging all about the room.

- Risk mitigation—Risk is an uncertain event that might affect your project. Reducing, or mitigating, risk is at the very root of agile because it encourages frequent delivery, adaptation to change, priority refinement, and constant inspection.

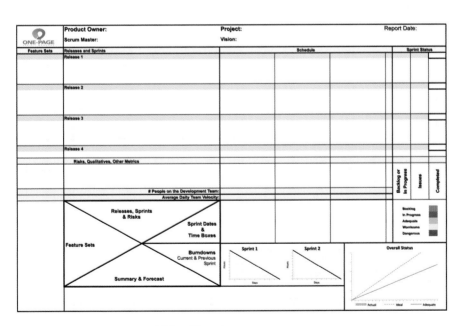

FIGURE 7.3   *The Agile OPPM Template*

Copyright OPPMi 2012. PDF color templates available at www.oppmi.com.

Figure 7.3, the Agile OPPM template, incorporates and illustrates the essential agile elements discussed above. Figures in Chapters 8 and 9 are from the Front Office portion of the O.C. Tanner Cornerstone ERP software implementation project.

The 12 Construction Steps for an Agile OPPM

Figure 7.2 in the previous chapter shows an agile one-page project manager (OPPM). The 12 steps needed to construct it are seen in Figure 8.1.

We will now create an agile OPPM.

STEP 1: THE HEADER

What It Is

The first step is to provide basic information about the project. This goes at the top of the form in the highlighted rectangle (Figure 8.2).

This information includes:

- Project: Cornerstone—Front Office
- Product Owner: Clark Campbell
- Scrum Master: Larrie Elkins

- Vision: Upgrade Sales Configuration System
- Report Date

How to Do It

This part of the agile OPPM is similar in construction to the traditional OPPM. A notable difference is the inclusion of a Scrum Master. Also, rather than referring to the objective and sub-objectives, with agile we have vision and feature sets.

As noted in the previous chapter, the vision is similar to a traditional objective but less definite with an expectation for change. This is where the product owner and often the Scrum Master meet with the boss to receive the project

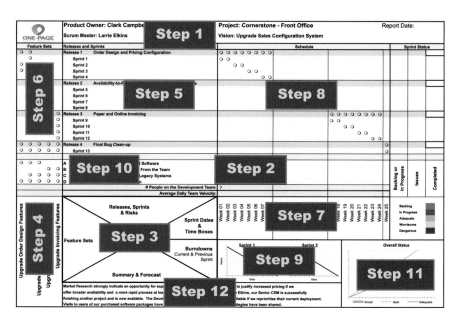

FIGURE 8.1   *The 12 Agile OPPM Construction Steps*

Copyright OPPMi 2012. PDF color templates available at www.oppmi.com.

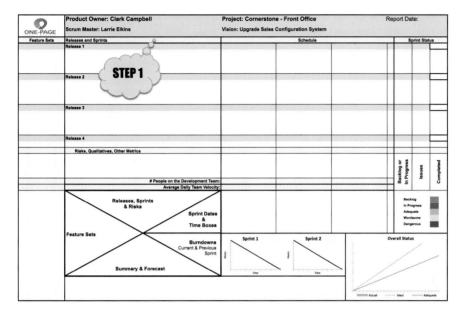

FIGURE 8.2   *Agile Step 1: The Header*

Copyright OPPMi 2012. PDF color templates available at www.oppmi.com.

assignment. In this example, the vision is to upgrade the sales configuration system.

Now is when conversations are held about the boss's expectations concerning the budget, time, and vision. There should be collaboration among the Scrum Master, the product owner, and the boss. Some organizations do not include the Scrum Master, but I advise that the Scrum Master be part of this meeting.

A word about the Scrum Master. Mountain Goat Software provides a good description of this position and its responsibilities:

The Scrum Master is responsible for making sure a Scrum team lives by the values and practices of Scrum.

The Scrum Master is often considered a coach for the team, helping the team do the best work it possibly can. The Scrum Master can also be thought of as a process owner for the team, creating a balance with the project's key stakeholder, who is referred to as the product owner.

Not worth repeating from our discussion about traditional methodology is the discussion about the project name because this is essentially the same as with the traditional OPPM. And the report date is not filled in because there is not yet a report.

STEP 2: DEVELOPMENT TEAM

What It Is

As seen on Figure 8.3, this is the team that will do the software development. As a general rule, Scrum teams should be permanently assigned to a project. This is important. In my experience, the optimal size of a team is between five and nine; in our example, the team has seven members who have been identified and assigned.

The OPPM reminds the product owner and the boss of their job to select the development team. Also desirable is having all team members in one location, if possible. You need to get approval of team members' supervisors to join the team. The extra effort often required securing the people you need and want most frequently guarantees a valuable return exceeding your near-term initial investment.

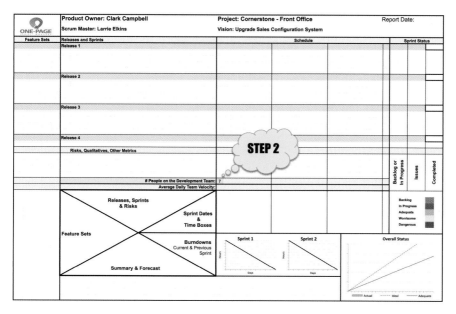

FIGURE 8.3   *Agile Step 2: The Development Team*
Copyright OPPMi 2012. PDF color templates available at www.oppmi.com.

How to Do It

Agile teams are generally smaller and work in much closer proximity than the various traditional project teams. The team needs sufficient skills within itself to accomplish the work. Teams are cross-functional and must be willing and able to become self-organizing.

STEP 3: THE MATRIX

What It Is

Figure 8.4 shows the matrix. The idea of the agile OPPM matrix is the same as that of the traditional OPPM; it is the hub of the OPPM where all points meet.

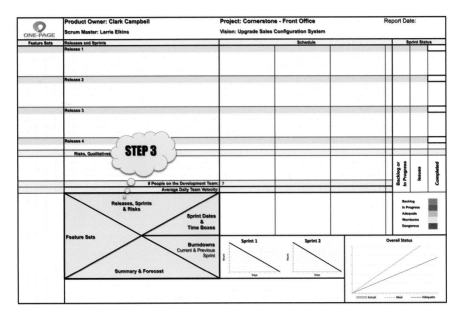

FIGURE 8.4   *Agile Step 3: The Matrix*

Copyright OPPMi 2012. PDF color templates available at www.oppmi.com.

How to Do It

As with the traditional OPPM, you will gather your team and start the discussion on how to handle this project. Both the product owner and the Scrum Master are responsible for two kinds of training:

1. Agile project training in general—namely, the techniques of agile project management
2. Agile OPPM training, where you teach the agile OPPM

If your team is experienced, you will likely need to teach the elements of the agile OPPM but not of agile project management in general. A less experienced team may need some training help from outside your organization and on how the agile OPPM works.

This is a good place to comment on the polarization that has occurred and, in some places, continues, between traditional and agile project management as agilists and traditionalists dramatize the differences in support of their organizations more popular approach. These debates can be valuable only if they lead to mutual understanding and the eventual blend of methods needed for many projects. Fewer and fewer projects today are purely traditional or purely agile. Wise managers strive to form just the right "hybrid" that works for their organization, talent, and types of projects.

Jim Highsmith, one of the original 17 Snowbird agilists who penned the Agile Manifesto and the 12 Agile Principles, writes in his book *Agile Project Management—Creating Innovative Products* (Boston: Addison-Wesley Professional, Pearson Education, 2009), "Traditional Project Managers tend to focus on requirements as the definition of scope, and then concentrate on delivering those requirements. Agile Project Leaders focus on delivering value and are constantly asking questions about whether different renditions of scope are worth the value they deliver."

STEP 4: FEATURE SETS
What It Is

Collaboration with customers reveals certain sets of features they find valuable.

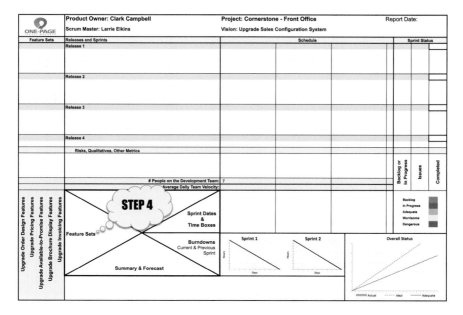

FIGURE 8.5   *Agile Step 4: The Feature Sets*
Copyright OPPMi 2012. PDF color templates available at www.oppmi.com.

In our previous example about developing a GPS, the feature sets are the picture of the road on the screen, male and female voices, and voices with various accents.

In the example seen in Figure 8.5, the feature sets are:

- Upgrade Order Design Features
- Upgrade Pricing Features
- Upgrade Available-to-Promise Features
- Upgrade Brochure Display Features
- Upgrade Invoicing Features

How to Do It

An agile project will have many features, or "chunks," of functionality envisioned to provide business value.

Every feature cannot be shown on an agile OPPM; therefore, your team, along with the customer, should look for commonality and group them into reasonable collections gathered under an umbrella of recognizable similarity.

STEP 5: RELEASES AND SPRINTS

What It Is

Release planning is collaboration between your customer and your development team. Once you have identified features and grouped them into feature sets, the development team estimates required effort as a baseline for prioritization. Story points or development hours are the most common variable; I confess a bias for using hours because they are more easily understood outside the agile project team.

   In agile/Scrum, a sprint is a repeatable work cycle, usually two to four weeks in length, during which time the team creates a shippable product. The product owner prioritizes the features and determines when to release. Each sprint builds iteratively on the previous sprints to incrementally deliver value to the customers. As in the example from the previous chapter, rather than providing the customer with one fully completed product, such as an airplane, agile methodology delivers small iterations of the product to the customer and does so frequently.

How to Do It

Sprints come out of your planning. You need to determine how many sprints you want in each release. Typically, sprints number 4 to 12 per release.

The example illustrated in Figure 8.6 has four releases, with the first three having four sprints apiece, whereas the last has but one sprint. With software, the last sprint is often a bug fix and has just one release. Bugs are generally fixed along the way in each sprint, sufficient that working software is delivered. Experience has shown that a concluding sprint just to clean up recently discovered or delayed non-critical bugs is good practice.

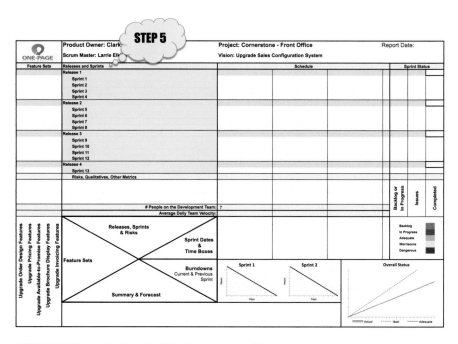

FIGURE 8.6   *Agile Step 5: The Releases and Sprints*

Copyright OPPMi 2012. PDF color templates available at www.oppmi.com.

STEP 6: ALIGNING SPRINTS WITH FEATURE SETS

What It Is

Here is where you utilize your high-level planning results to show which feature sets are planned for each sprint and release. Strong arguments can be made for only planning feature sets for one or two releases at time. The number of sprints and releases to be displayed on your OPPM depends on the planning experience of your team and the expectation of your boss and customers. This is illustrated in Figure 8.7.

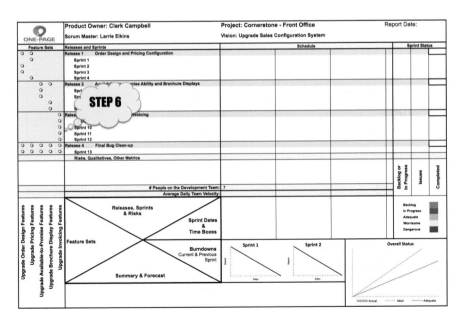

FIGURE 8.7   *Agile Step 6: Aligning Features to Releases and Sprints*

Copyright OPPMi 2012. PDF color templates available at www.oppmi.com.

143

How to Do It

Some people think no planning is necessary with agile. Quite the contrary. With agile, we have a plan, but it is a plan that gets adjusted along the way.

In the Cornerstone project, Release 1 is aligned with the feature sets: Upgrade Order Design Features and Upgrade Pricing Features. You can see this with the circles in the first line of Release 1. Below that, you can read which feature set relates to which sprint. Note that in the final release, Release 4, Final Bug Clean-up, all the feature sets relate to the final sprint, Sprint 13, because all the feature sets will go through a bug clean up.

STEP 7: SPRINT DATES AND TIME BOXES

What It Is

In our example, Figure 8.8, there are one-week time boxes; each sprint lasts two weeks. The planning horizon for our project is 25 weeks, and you can see there are 25 weekly boxes. We will report on our progress weekly.

How to Do It

The time horizon for an agile project means something quite different than the go-live date of a traditional project—not better or worse generally, just different. Traditional projects are best when technology is familiar and product requirements are stable or routine. Agile projects are best when technology is unfamiliar or

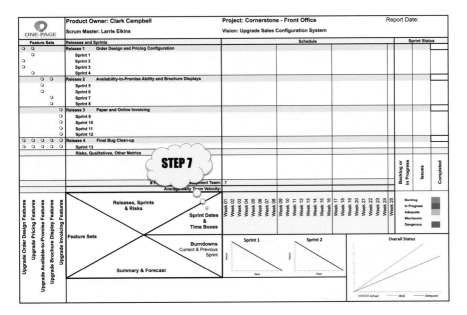

FIGURE 8.8   *Agile Step 7: Sprint Dates and Time Boxes*

Copyright OPPMi 2012. PDF color templates available at www.oppmi.com.

leading edge and product requirements are fluctuating or unpredictable.

As we mentioned in Chapter 5, before you commit to the completion date, think carefully about what you are committing to. With traditional projects, you are committing to a single on-time delivery of all the scope. With agile, you are committing to incrementally and frequently delivered working solutions for fixed periods.

STEP 8: THE SCHEDULE

What It Is

In Figure 8.9, we align the sprints and releases with the time boxes.

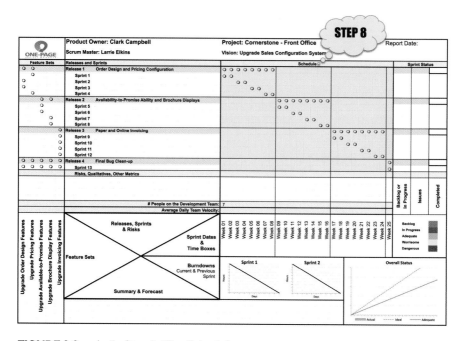

FIGURE 8.9   *Agile Step 8: The Schedule*

Copyright OPPMi 2012. PDF color templates available at www.oppmi.com.

How to Do It

This is a visual display of our sprint/release planning showing how many total sprints we plan and the number of sprints planned for each release. We place an empty circle in the boxes alongside the release. In our example, each release takes eight weeks. Release 1 (Order Design and Pricing Configuration) is scheduled for completion between Weeks 01 and 08; Release 2 (Availability-to-Promise Ability and Brochure Displays), between Weeks 09 and 16; and Release 3 (Paper and Online Invoicing), between Weeks 17 and 24. The last release, Release 4 (Final Bug Clean-up) is scheduled for one week.

On each release title line, empty circles are placed for each week because the release is expected to take that time represented by those circles. Below the title lines are the sprints, and each sprint is scheduled for two weeks. Sprint 1 is scheduled for Weeks 01 and 02; Sprint 2, for Weeks 03 and 04; Sprint 3, for Weeks 05 and 06; and so on. By looking at the OPPM, you can see graphically the start and stop dates of each release (Release 1, for example, starts on Week 01 and ends on Week 08) and the start and stop dates of each sprint. Easily and quickly, the reader sees how much time is being devoted to each release and sprint and when the release and sprints are scheduled to start and stop.

STEP 9: BACKLOG BURNDOWN

What It Is

This step (Figure 8.10) involves the two burndown charts planned to be shown on each OPPM. These graphical displays of development progress for each sprint could be applied to any project where progress can be measured over time; however, they are not generally applied to traditional projects and are one of the most important tools for the agile practitioners.

How to Do It

In this step we include in the OPPM the burndown chart for the previous sprint and the current sprint. They could be shown by release instead. This step is a good time

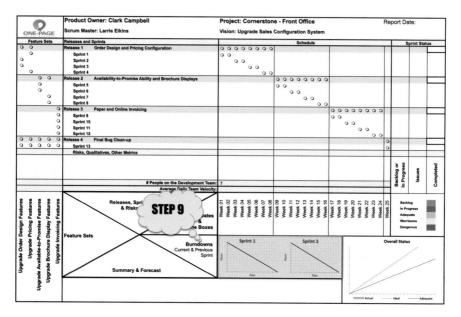

FIGURE 8.10   *Agile Step 9: The Burndown Charts*
Copyright OPPMi 2012. PDF color templates available at www.oppmi.com.

to carefully go over the value of burndown charts and expected input needed from your development team.

STEP 10: RISKS, QUALITATIVES, AND OTHER METRICS

What It Is

As we noted in our discussion of this step with the tradi-tional OPPM, this portion deals with subjective or quali-tative aspects of a project (Figure 8.11). Every project has aspects that do not easily lend themselves to quantitative analysis. What qualifies as acceptable performance with software is often difficult to say. A screen that comes up in one or two seconds may be acceptable — or not. A mod-est amount of customization may be acceptable — or not.

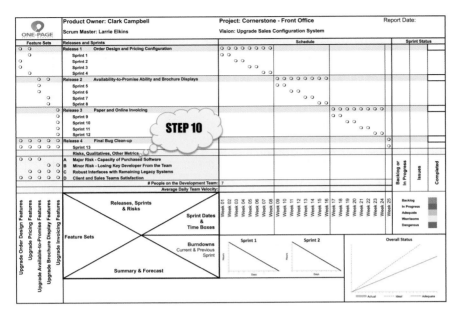

FIGURE 8.11   *Agile Step 10: Risks, Qualitatives, and Other Metrics*
Copyright OPPMi 2012. PDF color templates available at www.oppmi.com.

We report performance with stoplight colors red, yellow, and green.

How to Do It

Risks are aligned to feature sets. In Figure 8.11, Major Risk "A" relates to the Capacity of Purchased Software, and this, in turn, is aligned with the feature sets for Upgrade Order Design Features, Upgrade Pricing Features, and Upgrade Available-to-Promise Features.

The functionality of the legacy systems we replaced were far more complex than any of our software vendors anticipated. This, coupled with the new functionality demanded by both our internal and external customers, established requirements subject to failure. As you can

149

imagine, the usual debates over in-house development versus purchasing packaged software recognized this very real project risk.

Then there is the minor risk related to Losing a Key Developer From the Team because we were dependent on her intimate knowledge of the legacy systems she had designed and programmed. Other risks relate to Robust Interfaces with Remaining Legacy Systems and, most important, Client and Sales Teams Satisfaction.

STEP 11: OVERALL STATUS
What It Is

Figure 8.12, Overall Status, provides a status report for senior management and other stakeholders using a burnup chart. The burndown chart we just discussed shows how much backlog remains, whereas the burnup chart depicts how much has been accomplished and, overall, how well the project is progressing. Here, up is good and down is bad.

The solid line shows adequate performance, and the dotted line is the ideal. Agilists refer to the triangle formed by these two lines as the cone of happiness, because it is where you are pleased with your performance. The ideal line is usually about 10 percent better than your expected team velocity, whereas the adequate line could represent about 10 percent below. Therefore, if your performance is between these two lines, your burn rate is as expected.

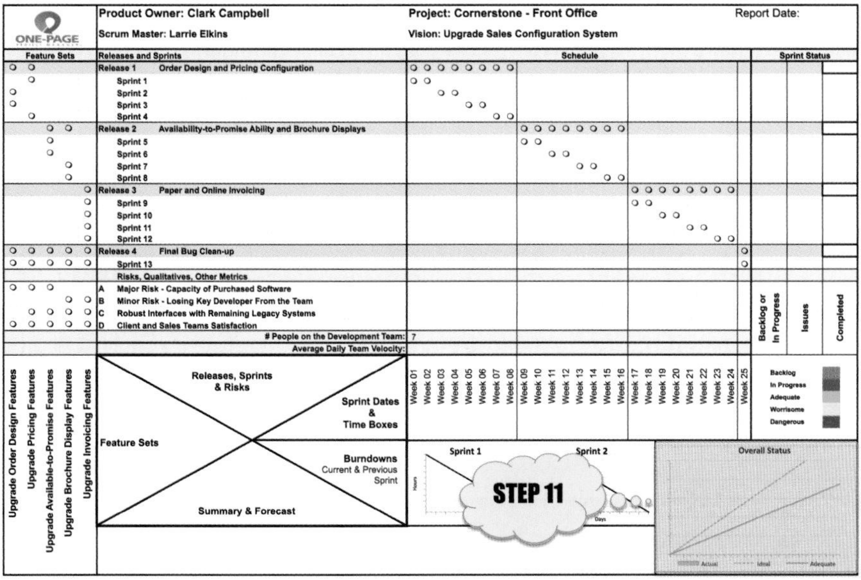

FIGURE 8.12   *Agile Step 11: Overall Status—Burnup Chart*
Copyright OPPMi 2012. PDF color templates available at www.oppmi.com.

How to Do It

As you will see in the next chapter, we will fill in this section of the OPPM with colored bars to create a chart that lets the reader know where we are in respect to these two status lines.

STEP 12: SUMMARY & FORECAST
What It Is

Your OPPM is now complete except for this section. Here is where you inform your readers how the project is doing and what you forecast for the immediate future.

How to Do It

Not much space is provided — for a reason. The OPPM, both the traditional and agile versions, are primarily graphic representations to take advantage of how succinctly a picture can describe a situation. If you write a long tome about a project and its progress, you negate the very strength of the OPPM.

For this reason, minimal space is provided for explanations. But it is understood that some description is often needed because the graphics cannot convey all important information. Such missing information belongs in this section. This is not a place to repeat what is already depicted elsewhere in the OPPM.

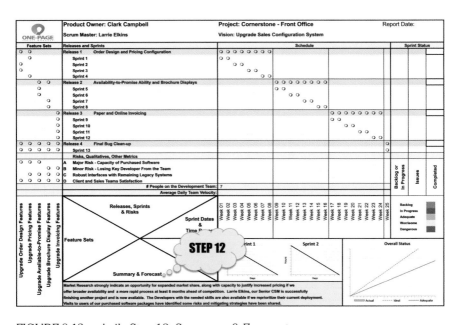

FIGURE 8.13   *Agile Step 12: Summary & Forecast*

Copyright OPPMi 2012. PDF color templates available at www.oppmi.com.

You can see how this is done in Figure 8.13, which reads as follows:

Market Research strongly indicates an opportunity for expanded market share, along with capacity to justify increased pricing if we offer broader availability and a more rapid process at least six months ahead of competition. Larrie Elkins, our Senior CSM, is successfully finishing another project and is now available. The Developers with the needed skills are also available if we reprioritize their current deployment. Visits to users of our purchased software packages have identified some risks and mitigating strategies have been shared.

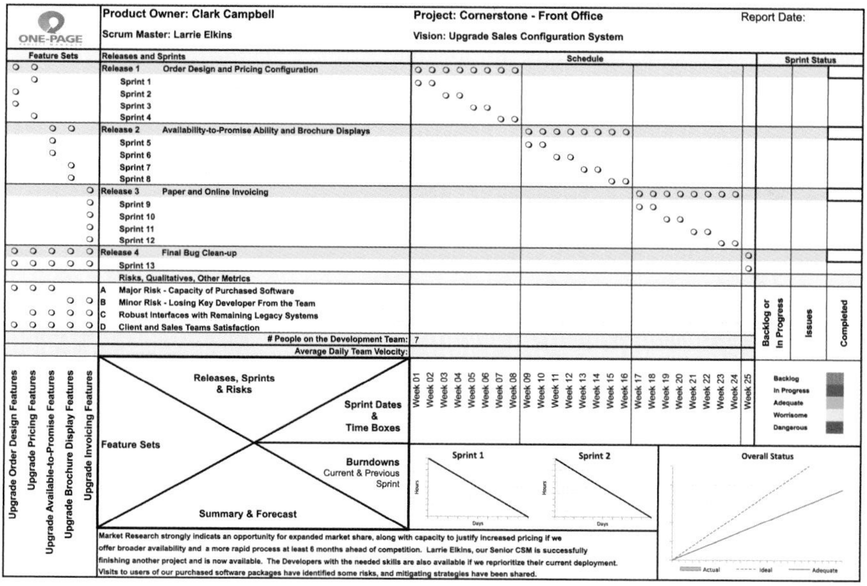

FIGURE 8.14   *Agile OPPM: The Cornerstone Front Office*
Copyright OPPMi 2012. PDF color templates available at www.oppmi.com.

Figure 8.14 is the final product of your agile planning and completion of the 12 agile OPPM construction steps. This single page communicates the plan and was submitted to management to receive funding and the go-ahead to launch the Cornerstone—Front Office Project.

The Seven Reporting Steps for an Agile OPPM

We are now ready to use the one-page project manager (OPPM) we just built. The project, which was introduced in the previous chapter, was part of a software project I managed at Tanner called Cornerstone, and it involved the deployment of SAP enterprise software for finance, manufacturing, supply chain, and a front office component. Chapter 6 of my second book, *The One-Page Project Manager for IT Projects,* discusses the main body of this project in detail. OPPMs were essential for this project and, we will present the front office piece in the agile OPPM format. Typical big bang traditional go-live challenges pressed us into the newly emerging agile methods. Shortly after the completion of the project that we will display in this chapter, O.C. Tanner was recognized by *CIO* magazine. Here is a quote from *IT Management News*, August 23, 2004:

> *O.C. Tanner Recognition Company has been named one of CIO Magazine's "Agile 100" for the company's ability to marry "IT agility with enterprise agility in order to move quickly, adapt intelligently and create advantage in a rapidly changing world," according to the publication.*
>
> *O.C. Tanner will be honored by the magazine's editors in Colorado Springs on Aug. 24, along with other leading companies such as FedEx Corp., T. Rowe Price, Dell, SBC, Harvard Business School and General Motors.*
>
> *O.C. Tanner was recognized for using agile software development methodology to implement more than 1,000 business system enhancements in a single year, and for IT enhancements to manufacturing, supply chain and customer-facing processes.*
>
> *"Beginning in early 2002, our Information Technology organization began the implementation of lean and agile methodologies that have substantially improved our organization's productivity and connection to the business," said David Berg, Senior Vice President and CIO.*

For purposes of illustration, I am showing the project at the end of Week 13 in Figure 9.1.

SEVEN STEPS TO CREATING A REPORT USING THE OPPM

You meet with your project's owners near the conclusion of each report date and complete the following tasks:

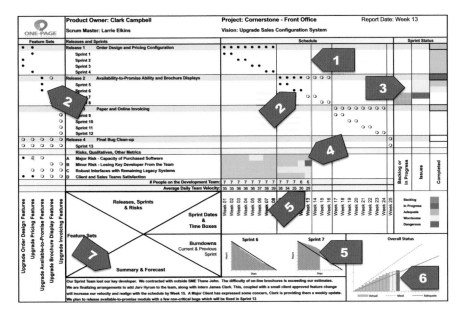

FIGURE 9.1   *The Seven Agile Reporting Steps*
Copyright OPPMi 2012. PDF color templates available at www.oppmi.com.

Step 1

Insert the red vertical line between Week 13 and Week 14, the current time. This lets the reader quickly know where on the project's timeline this OPPM is reporting on. Insert the report date in the upper right-hand corner.

Step 2

Fill in the dots as pointed to by the right-hand Number 2 arrow, which shows how well we are completing various sprints. Release 1 (Order Design and Pricing Configuration) is finished, as illustrated by all the bubbles being filled in. The far-left Number 2 arrow shows completion of the planned feature sets.

We are currently engaged in Release 2 (Availability-to-Promise Ability and Brochure Displays). This is illustrated by the dots relating to Release 2, which runs from Week 09 through Week 16. You can tell Release 1 is complete because all its dots are filled in, and you can tell Release 3 (Paper and Online Invoicing) has not started because the dots for this release do not begin until Week 17.

The dot for Release 2 just to the left of the vertical red line is not filled in, indicating there are issues with this release. You can see the challenge is with Sprint 7, whose dot should have been filled in this past week but is not. This sprint was not completed this week as scheduled. As a result, the feature set (left side), Upgrade Brochure Display Features, is suffering. Note, though, that this full feature set is not scheduled to be completed for another three weeks; the schedule calls for one more week to complete Sprint 7 and two weeks to complete Sprint 8.

Step 3

Arrow 3 refers to the Sprint Status report. Release 1 is green, meaning adequate, in the bolded box. This is saying the release was delivered, all sprints were accomplished well, and customers (internal and external) are satisfied with the results. You can find the meaning of the colors in the legend located below the Sprint Status report. The left-hand and middle column under Sprint Status are white for this release, indicating the backlogs have been emptied and no serious issues remain.

Release 2 has a bolded box filled in with blue, which means it is in progress. Sprint 5 had issues (which is why there is yellow in the Issues column), but under Completed, it is green, meaning good enough.

The backlog for Sprint 6 is completed, so it is white in the Backlog or In Progress column. However, it is yellow in the next two columns—Issues and Completed—which means we are concerned about that release. We decided to include this software in the planned Release 2 although we remain worried because of a few lingering issues.

Sprint 7 is filled in gray under the Backlog or In Progress column, indicating its features are waiting in the backlog for this sprint. Under Issues, there is a red box, indicating we are very worried about the performance.

Sprint 8 is gray under Backlog or In Progress, indicating no work has yet begun to reduce this posted backlog.

Release 3 is a gray box under Completion, which means we have a high-level planned backlog ready for Sprints 9 through 12 to tackle it.

Step 4

Here we are filling in the boxes under the Risks, Qualitatives, Other Metrics section. With A: Major Risk—Capacity of Purchased Software, we were concerned about it during Weeks 05 and 06 (when the boxes were filled in with yellow), but the remainder of the time the boxes are green, indicating performance was adequate. B: Minor Risk—Losing Key Developer From the Team has gone red this week. We were unable to retain this critical talent. C: Robust Interfaces with Remaining Legacy Systems started off well—the first eight weeks are green—but since then, we have been concerned. The final risk, D: Client and

Sales Team Satisfaction, has been consistently adequate until this week when it turned yellow, indicating we now have an issue with it.

Step 5

There are two Number 5 arrows. The upper one tells you the Average Daily Team Velocity. As I noted in Chapter 7, *team velocity* refers to the amount of work your development team can accomplish in a day and is calculated by counting the number of units of work completed during a specified time interval. In the past week, the velocity was only 29 hours, the lowest it has been since the start of the Cornerstone project; it peaked in Week 08, when it hit 39. This means the team accomplished less in Week 13 than in

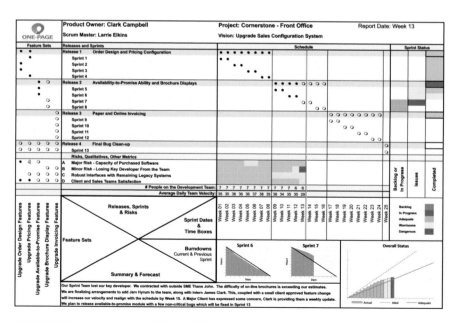

FIGURE 9.2   *Front Office Week 13 Report*

Copyright OPPMi 2012. PDF color templates available at www.oppmi.com.

any other week and is reflected in Step 3 and the red box
we discussed under Sprint Status—Sprint 7 and in Step 4
with the red and yellow boxes.

The lower arrow points to the burndown chart, which
shows, day by day, the amount of work remaining in
Sprints 6 and 7 relative to the amount of time remaining.
Sprint 6 started off on schedule, then ran for several weeks
ahead of schedule (this is shown by the gray area being
below the planned burndown line) and then returned
to completing the planned work for that sprint. However,
Sprint 7 shows the gray area above the line, indicating the
backlog is not being "burned" down as planned.

Step 6

With this step, we are looking at the Overall Status of the
project. This is telling us two different but related stories.
One story is found in the colors of the bars. For the first 10
weeks, the bars were all green—the project was progressing at least adequately, if not better. Weeks 11 and 12 are
shaded in yellow, an indication the project was running
into some difficulty. And the last week, Number 13, is in
red, which tells us we are moving into an area of serious
difficulty.

The second story provides a more encompassing view.
Look at the cone of happiness—the area between the
lines representing the ideal and the adequate. Even with
the challenges of the past three weeks, we are still inside
the cone of happiness. Admittedly, four weeks ago we
were well within it and now, in Week 13, we are on the

edge of falling below what we considered adequate. One of the great values of the agile OPPM is that it gives off early warning signals. Yes, things were progressing nicely for about three months, but now we have serious issues. Figure 9.2 shows the Week 13 report without the step arrows.

Step 7

The Summary & Forecast explains why things are happening. In the last week, we've seen Sprint 7 falling behind, a couple Risks becoming yellow and one turning to red, and the Overall Status being labeled red.

What is going on now in the Cornerstone project? The explanation is found in this last section. Here we learn the project lost its key developer, which explains why the Average Team Velocity is now at its lowest point. What are we doing about it? We learn that here, too, by seeing that subject matter expert Thane John has been hired and that arrangements are being finalized to add Jarv Hyrum to the team along with intern James Clark. And, as it says in this section, "This, coupled with a small client approved feature change will increase our velocity and realign with the schedule by Week 15." We learn here that steps have been taken to handle the challenges and we expect to be back on track within two weeks.

We also learn that the difficulty relating to online brochures is exceeding estimates. In addition, a major client has expressed some concern about the project and Clark is handling this issue directly by providing the client with a weekly update. Finally, this section lets us know we plan to release the available-to-promise module with a few noncritical bugs, which will be fixed in Sprint 13 (the sprint dedicated to cleaning up remaining bugs).

Figure 9.3 shows the Agile OPPM status for Week 24, one week prior to the planned completion of the project.

The bottom right burnup chart shows a nice recovery from the mid-project challenges. Releases 1 and 3 were okay, and features from Release 2 work but still have issues. Red boxes revealed serious software capacity issues surfacing in Weeks 18 through 20 but are now resolved. The string of yellow boxes tells a chronic story of worrisome interface performance. The final bug cleanup sprint is in progress and is yellow.

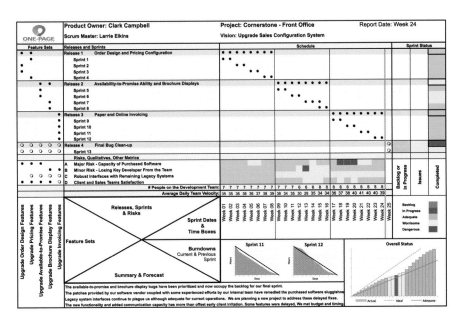

FIGURE 9.3   *The Cornerstone — Front Office Week 24 Report*

Copyright OPPMi 2012. PDF color templates available at www.oppmi.com.

The questions posed by the Week 24 OPPM are answered with the following in the Summary & Forecast:

The available-to-promise and brochure display bugs have been prioritized and now occupy the backlog for our final sprint.

The patches provided by our software vendor coupled with some experienced efforts by our internal team have remedied the purchased software sluggishness.

Legacy system interfaces continue to plague us although adequate for current operations. We are planning a new project to address these delayed fixes.

The new functionality and added communication capacity have more than offset early client irritation. Some features were delayed; we met budget and timing.

Finally, many agilists would suggest that as we approach the end of the project, the most important single piece of information communicated by this Agile OPPM is *Client Satisfaction* as displayed by the last four contiguous weekly greens on line D of the Risks section.

CHAPTER 10

Thinking about Projects

This chapter is based solely on our observations and no claim is made to psychological, academic, or clinical expertise in organizational behavior. We have all read about right-brained versus left-brained predisposition, about multiple intelligences, and about intelligence quotient (IQ) and emotional quotient (EQ). In our training seminars, we have asked more than a thousand project managers how they approach project planning. Does their mind go to the start and work forward, or does it go to the end and work backward? Or do they randomly envision the interrelated elements?

We mentioned earlier the Harvard Mentor series book on project management. The authors propose a three-by-two construct for communicating effectively. We have labeled this the Harvard 3-by-2 and added it to our communication toolbox along with the one-page project manager (OPPM) and Andy Crowe's Alpha Four.

The Harvard 3-by-2 outlines effective project communication as:

1. Efficient and sufficient
2. Candid and timely
3. Explaining why and what's next

The OPPM seeks to support each of these three pairs. Candid, timely, why and what's next are relatively clear concepts and project managers have little difficulty determining how to bring their communication in line with each.

Balancing efficiency with sufficiency is much more challenging, different for every project, and changing with every stakeholder, and it is critical that we get it right.

Applying the theory, principles, and practices presented in Chapter 1 will help us deal with our "detail syndrome." We add here one more visual. Sorry, it is about sports, but it is more than a metaphor; it is a real-life example of balancing efficiency with sufficiency. And, being a visual display, we tend to remember the relationships and think how they might be applied to communicating about our progressing projects.

I invite my college students, and Mick invites his seminar learners, to construct visuals of project management principles. This one emerged from a group of seasoned project professionals, one of whom was an NFL referee.

Figures 10.1 and 10.2 were their creations. We have used them, with generous attribution, ever since.

Imagine watching your favorite football team in their most important game of the year. The score is tied and time is running out. Your wide receiver races down the sideline to catch a pass thrown long into the end zone. He and his defender are bumping and pushing each other as they leap, arms and hands outstretched to the limit. He grasps the ball with his fingertips just a whisker above the turf. The back judge hesitates, then signals incomplete pass.

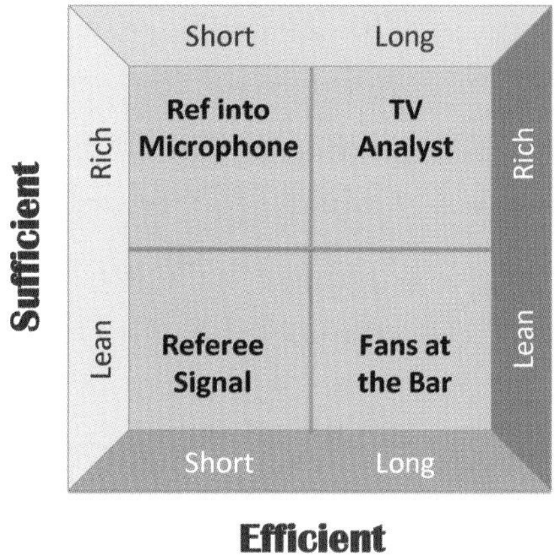

Now consider Figure 10.1. The bottom horizontal axis represents efficiency, from short messages to long conversations. The vertical axis represents sufficiency, with knowledgeable content rising from lean to rich. Each of the four boxes represents communication that is a little incomplete, a little out of balance. The bottom left reflects what the referee's signal communicates—very short, very lean, no catch, and no touchdown. As the instant replays are being considered,

FIGURE 10.1   *Efficient versus Sufficient Communication Challenge*
Copyright OPPMi 2012.

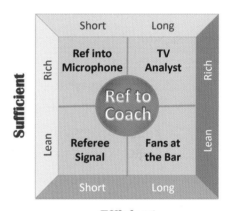

FIGURE 10.2   *Efficient versus Sufficient Communication Sweet Spot*
Copyright OPPMi 2012.

you listen to the TV analysts fill the airtime with long conversations peppered with their rich understanding of the game. This is displayed at the top right corner. At the same time, in the local bar, fans, represented at the bottom right corner, argue loud and long with a somewhat tipsy absence of full understanding. The referee puts on his headphones and listens to the decision of the replay official. He walks onto the field, clicks his microphone, and with a sufficiently rich understanding of the facts and the rules, makes a short announcement.

When communicating about your project, a short/lean message like "We are on time," a short/rich message like "Our CPI and SPI are both greater than 1.0," a long/rich status report book, or a long/lean commentary by a casual observer are each incomplete and out of balance.

At the center of Figure 10.2 is a balance between efficiency and sufficiency—a sweet spot—representing when the referee goes to the sideline and explains the call to the head coach of the receiver. Each participant in this "critical conversation" has a deep and rich knowledge of the rules and the observed infraction. For both, the stakes are high, and they are limited in the time they can spend in this communication.

Comments from Readers and Users

The OPPM is a very concise way of reporting a lot of info in a very easy to understand, single-page report. Looking forward to implementing this at DFW.

—R. Bee, Dallas Fort Worth Airport, August 5, 2011

OPPMs have found their way into the communication sweet spot for many organizations. Efforts to achieve the right balance between efficiency and sufficiency are worth it because effective communication is the single most valuable contribution of the best, and indeed every, project manager.

Before starting any project, the project leader is faced with what is often the most difficult decision concerning the entire endeavor: who to put on the project team. It's like cooking: if your ingredients are poor, no matter how wonderful the recipe and how carefully you follow the instructions, the end result will be wanting. But get superior ingredients, and you are more ensured of a delicious result.

The same thing holds true for project teams. My experience is that project team members think differently in some very fundamental ways. I don't mean this in a denigrating way; each of us has strengths and weaknesses. Albert Einstein was a great physicist, but that doesn't mean he was a wonderful athlete. Bill Gates is an innovative genius, but I doubt he is a great violinist. Michael Jordan could play basketball like no one else, but baseball was another matter.

I have identified three types of people who, when brought together, create an ideal mix for managing any type of project, traditional or agile. Some people fit into two of these types (few have all three attributes). Figure 10.3 shows how these types can overlap. They are the ingredients you need to help ensure your project team is successful. When you have these types represented on

FIGURE 10.3   *Three Types of Thinkers*

your project team, you have all the strengths you need and the ability to override any notable weaknesses. Let's look at these three types.

THE VISIONARY THINKER

Visionaries are generally your brightest and most creative team members. They are out-of-the-box thinkers, they think about things in novel ways, and they can dive deeply into a subject or think across a wide range of subjects. They're not encumbered with the structure of how things are. They turn things upside down, and twist and turn them in new and unique combinations. The information technology (IT) world enjoys a particular concentration of visionaries, and agile itself is a visionary approach.

As a project manager, be aware that it is absolutely essential to have visionary thinkers on your team. They may sometimes create unique difficulties, but they amplify the deliverables of a project and enhance and augment a project's outcome.

They find solutions to intractable problems. They challenge conventional thinking and are less encumbered by groupthink. You will often hear them say, "Why not . . . " or "How about . . . " I cannot imagine a robust project team without visionaries.

Even though innovative visionaries are essential to a strong project team, as with every type of thinker, they come with unique challenges. The liability of visionaries is they are not focused much on the commercialization or the actual completion of the work. Once they've completed thinking through a problem, they are on to the next thought. They generate lots of ideas, but others must implement them. So as you proceed forward on your project planning before the project actually begins, know which of the visionary's ideas to incorporate and which to leave unused because you cannot use them all. Once the project has begun, the visionary's liability is scope creep. This means they are always ready with ideas—saying, "Oh, let's add this" or "Let's tweak that"—but they can come up with so many ideas and expand your project in so many ways that it never gets done. The more agile your project methods are, the more the visionaries' weaknesses turn into strengths.

Here's one other thought about intelligent visionaries: attempts to motivate by recognizing and appreciating their *efforts* is substantially more effective than praising their intellectual gifts. This seems particularly applicable following a series of failures. Those acknowledged for effort seem measurably more resilient and continuously engaged than those whose intellect is overstressed.

171

THE START-TO-FINISH THINKER

Todd Skinner, a talented and gritty mountain climber and professional speaker, taught his listeners about "getting on the wall." His experience in free climbing many of the most challenging vertical ascents in the world taught him that the time eventually arrives when planning must be declared adequate and climbing started. And, more important, by "getting on the wall," you learn what you never could have learned any other way—you *become* capable.

Start-to-finish thinkers on projects are get-on-the-wall types. They are anxious to get going and start doing. They think about what they need to do first and then get started. They believe they are not fully capable when they start but become capable as they progress, so the sooner they start, the better—a fundamental agile idea.

This approach is based on the belief that you can't know all that will happen or plan for every contingency. If you wait until you get all the answers, you'll never start. The start-to-finish thinker is anxious to get going, to get on the wall. Building the initial OPPM starts at the beginning. They reason: "We need to start with this, and then move on to that ... and then that ... " until complete. You may soon find them losing a little focus as the planning becomes increasingly granular or prolonged.

As a general rule, they are not particularly outstanding delegators. They have learned they do things well. They are confident. They are highly effective individual contributors. Handing off work to others is difficult. They may even feel some level of guilt when delegating to others what they themselves could do.

Start-to-finish thinkers are essential to a team because of the energy they bring and their focus on the task. You want them because of all the things they're focused on. They work to meet deadlines. The visionary concentrates on a project's scope, often venturing beyond; the start-to-finish player thinks about how to complete the task on time.

THE FINISH-TO-START THINKER

You will find finish-to-start thinkers in the libraries of any major college. They have their pencils lined up, their calendars telling them when to study for every class, and their books in order.

On a project team, they picture in their mind every project in its finished form. They know what a project will look like when it is done. With the OPPM, they start with the end in mind and build tasks and timelines backward to the beginning.

These are your best planners. They construct the OPPM right to left rather than left to right. Once all the tasks have been identified, they think about filling in the circles. This is in contrast to the visionary thinker, who doesn't think about circles or dots at all. The start-to-finish thinker starts filling in circles left to right: this is done first, this is done second, this is done third, and so on. The finish-to-start thinker fills in the plan right to left: if this is the finished product, then to complete it we have to have completed this, and before that we have to complete that. They go backward and, as a result, often end up with a longer time-line than the start-to-finish thinker.

The weakness of finish-to-start thinkers is they can overplan—the proverbial paralysis by analysis. They do not get on the wall soon enough; they wait and wait to get started. The start-to-finish thinker says, "Give me a couple of ducks," and then is off. The finish-to-start thinker wants all ducks in a row first.

My wife, Meredith, is a start-to-finish thinker, and I am a finish-to-start thinker. As such, we nicely complement (or clash with) each other. We had a home remodeling project where I did the planning and worried about which were the load-bearing walls and what needed to be done. I planned and planned. But the weakness of thinkers like me eventually came through, and nothing was getting done. I was undergoing paralysis by analysis. One day I returned home to find Meredith had taken a sledgehammer to a wall and reduced it to rubble. She had enough of my planning and figured it was time to start doing. She did more than "get on the wall"; she took down the wall.

A team of all finish-to-start thinkers will overplan your project, and be assured, they will not overspend the budget. But the timeline—well, that's another story.

Many IT people have found success in this type of thinking. They have learned to "start with the end in mind." For IT projects, however, the "end" is difficult and costly to fully specify because users can't completely identify everything they will need. Therefore, experienced chief information officers often partition larger projects into more definable chunks. They use agile methods by bounding both the scope and the timeline into more manageable chunks (called releases); a propensity for finish-to-start thinking is constrained to limiting the planning time. This also provides for some early deliverables while ignoring for the time being scope that may expand in a future chunk.

Another proven method for addressing these challenges is the path-based approach explored by Harvard professor David Upton (see "Radically Simple IT," *Harvard Business Review*, March 2008, by David M. Upton and Bradley R. Staats).

I have generally found that finish-to-start thinkers have, as a strength, a natural inclination to delegate and are comfortable surrounding themselves with people who are more competent than they are. They think about what processes or systems are needed for a project and who the best people are to accomplish what is needed, and they can be fearless at going out and getting them.

ASSETS OF THESE THINKERS

- The visionary thinker will ensure *innovation* and creativity.
- The start-to-finish thinker gets you moving, brings a "can do" attitude, and is passionate for the *timeline*.
- The finish-to-start thinker will be sure the project is well planned and stays on *budget*.

LIABILITIES OF THESE THINKERS

- The visionary guarantees *scope creep* to a traditional project, which affects both cost and the timeline. However, scope creep is not always bad.
- The start-to-finish thinker may paint you into a corner by starting things before they are fully thought out, requiring additional money and resources either not planned for or required to *reverse and repair.*
- The finish-to-start thinker is slow to begin and may allow the *timeline to slip*, especially in the early planning phase. This is a greater risk for longer projects.

PEOPLE ARE MULTIDIMENSIONAL

People are not one-dimensional. They are multidimensional and possess varying degrees of each type of thinking in their approach to projects. Generally, one type tends to dominate, however.

A few remarkable project leaders are in the triangle in the middle of Figure 10.3. They fire on all pistons, are bright and intuitive, have all sorts of ideas, and jump into a project right away with just the right amount of planning. These are unusual animals.

People who have strengths as visionary and start-to-finish thinkers will get a lot of things started but suffer some false starts. They have a pile of books on their nightstand, all partially read. They are good at starting things but often lose interest before the project is completed. They are bored easily and crave the thrill of starting something new.

Visionary and finish-to-start thinkers can really slow down a project. They plan things to death and are usually quite risk averse. They visualize how they want to finish a project and then envision a new, more expansive conclusion.

Those who combine finish-to-start and start-to-finish thinking are rare. Give them a set of plans, and they're off doing and accomplishing. On a vacation, they have everything planned. They know what they are going to do each day. They may miss, however, some unique opportunities or unusual activities only contemplated by the creative, visionary thinker.

WHAT THE PROJECT LEADER NEEDS TO DO

The project leader needs all types of thinkers on the project team. This way, the leader can tap the strengths of all of them. The leader also must understand which people are one-dimensional or two-dimensional (the three-dimensional person is so rare you'll have no trouble knowing who they are). In the simplest of terms, you need the visionary for the project's scope, the start-to-finish thinker for your timeline, and the finish-to-start thinker for your budget.

If you think about the people in your organization in terms of these three types of thinkers, you'll probably be able to quickly identify who fits into each category. Start-to-finish thinkers are all about getting things going, finish-to-start thinkers are all about careful planning, and visionary thinkers are all about possibilities.

Pure finish-to-start thinkers are good collaborators. Pure start-to-finish thinkers are quickly engaged. Pure visionaries are not good team members because no one can think as fast as they can. They don't work well on committees; instead, they work within their own minds. Nonetheless, you need all three types on your team.

Traditional and agile projects will each be richly rewarded by engaged people who think differently.

How do you identify who is who in your company? Walk around your office at 5:00 in the afternoon. The visionaries are alone. They are probably sitting in a chair reading a technical journal or just thinking. Or perhaps they are huddled over their computer keyboards writing. This is their private time. They are pondering.

The start-to-finish thinkers are busily working. There is paper all over the place; they are fully engaged. The finish-to-start thinkers have an office filled with people. They are writing on whiteboards, discussing things, and working things out. They are working with their collaborators, planning things, and thinking things through.

No one is good at everything. You need a team with visionary thinkers, start-to-finish thinkers, finish-to-start thinkers, and those who are multidimensional. A team with all of these attributes has great strength, and it can deal with all types of weakness. This is a team that can make the most of the OPPM and be most successful at completing your project.

The Project Management Office

Two elements of execution, as defined by Larry Bossidy and Ram Charan in their book *Execution — The Discipline of Getting Things Done* (New York: Crown Business, 2002), are

- A discipline of meshing strategy with reality, aligning people with goals, and achieving the results promised
- The way to link the three core processes of any business—the people process, the strategy process, and the operating plan—together to get things done on time

We have found in our teaching, consulting, and personal management experience that a powerful and effective project management office (PMO) using one-page project managers (OPPMs) provides the necessary champion and cohesive catalyst required to mesh strategy with execution, align people to plans, and therefore link people to strategy to action — and it allows it to be done in a "seriously simple" way.

Every project is run from some place. A small project could be run from someone's desk and might be one of several responsibilities of that person. Or a project could be coordinated from a central office devoted exclusively to corporate project communication. Or a very large project could have its own office.

The PMO is the person or group of people who have at least eight high-level, company-wide project responsibilities, all focused on seeing that projects are set up and managed for success.

This chapter is about how the PMO can use the OPPM effectively to address each of these eight project responsibilities.

PROJECT DASHBOARD

The first responsibility of the PMO is to maintain the dashboard for the organization's projects. The PMO tracks, at a high level, the progress of projects and reports them to upper management. This is a vital responsibility of the PMO. It reports to the company's executives in a way that allows them to know what is going on with projects and when attention is needed. The PMO keeps senior management fully aware, at a high level, of these basic areas:

- *The owners:* who are those responsible for various parts of a project

- *The cost:* how much the project has and will cost and whether it is currently on budget or off budget and by how much
- *The tasks:* how the deliverables and activities of the project are progressing versus the plan
- *The timeline:* when various project tasks are finished or are expected to be completed
- *The objectives:* the what (what the project is) and the why (why it is being done)

The PMO communicates these aspects of projects to executives for as long as the projects are under development or being completed. The OPPM's role in the PMO is as a tool that efficiently communicates essential information from the PMO to senior management. We don't think it is an overstatement to say the OPPM is *essential* to an effective PMO. It is essential because it consolidates all important information in one place. It is a critical communication link between a company's projects and its senior leaders. Think of it as the means by which information flows into and out of a PMO. And the OPPM manages that information by putting it into a form that's easily created, read, and understood. Without the OPPM, the PMO will be inundated with too much information. Moreover, its reporting output will be crisp and consolidated into a single OPPM. It is the *dashboard.*

The OPPM makes possible the PMO's ability to collect, analyze, and report a massive amount of project information. It facilitates the operational efficiency and the communication effectiveness of the PMO. By requiring every manager to report with the OPPM, you get only one page from each. It's a winnowing and summarization and the underpinning standard of excellence for a PMO.

CORPORATE PROJECT METHODOLOGY

The second important responsibility of the PMO is to be the keeper of the flame, the czar of the company's corporate project methodology. It must also provide tools to support that methodology. Furthermore, the PMO is responsible for project management systems. The value of the OPPM is, in effect, the communication system. The PMO uses the OPPM as the methodology for reporting and communicating about projects. The PMO ensures that every project manager knows how to use the OPPM. Without going too far in making claims for the tool, the OPPM helps promote professionalism in project management within an organization. It provides a protocol from which the discipline of project management can be reinforced.

PROJECT TRAINING

Third, the PMO has the responsibility to train and mentor project managers as they develop their skills. For example, our goal at O.C. Tanner is to have at least 95 percent of our people trained on and using the OPPM at any given time. We do this by having our project managers and those who work on projects read *The One-Page Project Manager*, receive general and specific training about the tool from project managers who have worked with the tool, and generally get encouragement from the PMO to use the tool. Of course, it helps that they experience the tool firsthand and discuss its use over time. This allows users to become more familiar and comfortable with it.

In addition to training on the OPPM, other reading materials, lectures, and seminars are provided to drive an expanding working knowledge of all aspects of project management's "body of knowledge."

CONSISTENT APPLICATION

The PMO ensures the consistent application of the methodology. This takes energy because people want to depart from the standard the organization establishes. Users think they have ways to improve the OPPM or that their project is so special it needs its own version of the OPPM. The PMO needs to manage such tendencies. It's not that the OPPM cannot be improved or should not be modified for specific situations, but such changes must be done at a high level to prevent balkanization of the tool. If left unchecked, such tendencies will lead, in short order, to many different OPPM formats, thereby losing the power of standardization and consistency.

The PMO must balance a standard methodology against continuous improvement. There is real value in consistency. It helps reinforce in the minds of users the value of the tool. It keeps project managers and team members focused on what is important. It makes it easier for everyone in the organization to learn how to create, use, and interpret the tool. The right balance between consistency and creativity yields efficiency and excellence.

It also helps management understand what the tool is communicating. Imagine an organization with many projects, each with its fundamentally different OPPM. Senior management will have to decipher what each version of the OPPM is trying to communicate, which negates much of the benefit of having a simple and consistent tool used across an organization with relatively minor variations for different types of projects. The bottom line: **the OPPM is the PMO's single most important communication tool**.

Keep in mind that for large projects the OPPM does not eliminate, replace, or substitute for any tool your project managers want to use, such as Microsoft Project or Oracle's Primavera software. It is in addition to the tools you are already using. A major project may have an OPPM at the top and then, drilling down, additional OPPMs for various aspects of the project. With a software project, we might use one OPPM for the hiring of a consultant, another for choosing the software, another for the limited rollout and testing of the software, and so on. At the top is an OPPM that reports on all those under it. It is this top-most OPPM that senior management sees.

The head of projects needs to strike a balance between standardization and customization. What this executive must be on guard for is the tendency of the user to customize the OPPM to the point where it is dramatically different from one project to another or from one department to another. Certain things *must* remain the same, such as the colors used (and their meanings), the use of empty circles to convey an aspect of a project not yet completed, and a filled-in circle that signifies completion.

However, some aspects of the tool can be changed. For example, some projects may use time periods of one week each, whereas others use monthly periods. Some OPPMs may incorporate graphs or charts, whereas others will not. It's the job of the head of the PMO to exercise the judgment necessary to maintain standards while allowing creativity, individual ownership, and innovation.

It's important to understand that the PMO produces a consolidated OPPM that is a summary of all the projects the office is tracking. The project managers for each project submit their OPPMs to the PMO, where they are, in turn, summarized onto a consolidated OPPM, which is essentially an OPPM that lists all current and recently completed projects. In this way, senior management quickly sees the status of all the projects happening in the organization. If they want more information about individual projects, they can read the OPPMs for those projects, often precluding inefficient inquiry with the project team.

PROJECT PUBLIC RELATIONS

We've talked a lot about how the OPPM communicates *up* an organization to senior management, but it also is able to communicate to those within or outside the organization who might have a tangential interest in the particular project. The PMO can use the tool to market and communicate aspects of a project *out* to audiences who might have a need to know about the project but are not intimately involved with it. Its simplicity makes it a great tool for such communication. Examples of outward audiences to whom the OPPM communicates include suppliers, other managers within the company, the company's human resources department (which wants to keep track of who is working on what projects), the internal audit department, and the sales department (which wants a quick look at how things are progressing on new products so it knows when new products will become available).

By the way, the OPPM has an additional benefit that might not be immediately obvious—namely, it can shorten management meetings. Because everyone is reading from the same page, both literally and metaphorically, when the PMO holds meetings, participants quickly get up to speed about the essential aspects of the project. This is a real time-saver. Many management meetings are too long. With the OPPM, you can reference back to the tool because everyone knows and understands it. Attention is keen when issues are germane to a person's area of responsibility. When other issues are perused, interest may dissipate. The OPPM helps make discussions clear, concise, and to the point, which is key to keeping everyone engaged.

PROJECT PRIORITIZATION

The OPPM helps the PMO prioritize its portfolio of projects. When the PMO compiles an OPPM that includes all projects, those that make it onto the tool automatically get priority. They get funded. They get resources ahead of other projects.

The OPPM also makes clear the demands that various projects are making on an organization. When a project appears on the corporate OPPM and the reader sees the project involves 300 people, or however many, it reminds everyone of the burden of certain projects and the load these projects are placing on various departments and the organization as a whole. The tool allows management to see the money and people being devoted to various projects and the need to balance the use of those and other resources with the day-to-day activities of the business. It's often difficult to keep projects and the daily demands of running a business in proper perspective. Projects are undertaken to make tomorrow's customer orders better, but this may come at the expense of today's orders. The OPPM, because it paints such a clear, readily accessible picture of projects, helps management keep a balance between now and the future.

PROJECT REVIEW AND CORRECTIVE ACTION

The consolidated OPPM facilitates the PMO's and senior management's attention to needed corrective action. The PMO conducts project reviews prior to reporting on those projects. The OPPM causes the PMO and the project team to think about the important aspects of a project. Sure, teams will think about timelines and budgets regardless of whether they use the OPPM, but they don't often think about who the owners are for each part of a project or how various parts of a project relate to important objectives or strategic goals. The OPPM makes these important connections readily apparent.

By using the OPPM, you and your team will have to think about all the essential elements of a project in addition to relationships between parts of the project and the people involved with it. And because the OPPM saves time, you will have the time to do this type of thorough planning. The work of the PMO ends up being more complete and effective because of the OPPM. One more thing: because the OPPM ties performance to individuals (the owners), when things go well, senior management can see it on the OPPM and take action, such as giving a compliment or otherwise providing positive recognition. The tool helps energize a whole culture of recognition, not just corrective action.

PROJECT ARCHIVES AND CONTINUOUS IMPROVEMENT

By holding onto the OPPMs for each project, which is easy to do because even a large project probably has an OPPM generated once a month (which is only 12 pages for a one-year project), the PMO is able to easily create and maintain an archive of completed projects.

These OPPMs become a repository of project learning. As George Santayana famously said, "Those who cannot learn from history are doomed to repeat it." Such an archive is a means by which future project leaders and teams can learn. It shows how things were done, how projects progressed, where challenges occurred, and how they were overcome. Using the OPPM to create a history is easy and efficient. And when a project is completed, the PMO just needs to have all the OPPMs bound and placed in a file cabinet, with electronic copies easily stored and retrieved.

EXAMPLE

The PMO provides a monthly report to management and other stakeholders, which contains the current OPPM for each strategic project. A summary OPPM showing the performance of all projects serves as the cover page. This summary OPPM for the PMO must communicate for each corporate project:

- Alignment with company strategy
- Correlation to the annual operating plan
- Capital budget tracking
- Expense budget tracking
- People involved
- Current performance or status
- On time versus lateness
- Assigned project manager
- Executive team responsibilities
- A consolidation and summation

This is the heart of the communication network.

Figure 11.1 is a general template. It is constructed to be able to incorporate both traditional projects and agile projects on a single page.

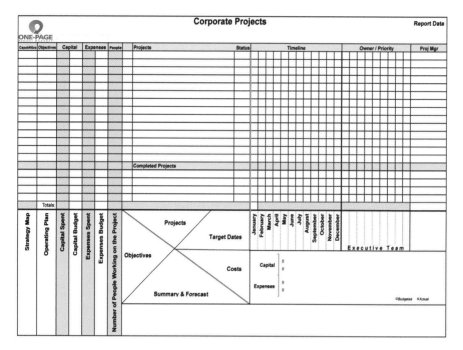

FIGURE 11.1 *The PMO OPPM Template*

Copyright OPPMi 2012. PDF color templates available at www.oppmi.com.

Figure 11.2 is an example from the fictitious Mount Olympus Company. Let's jump right into reading the November year-to-date report.

Look at the fourth heading from the left, Expenses. At the bottom of the two columns under Expenses are the labels Actual Expenses and Expenses Budget. The first reports what has actually been spent, whereas the second reports on the amount budgeted, or what was expected to be spent. The fifth line down in Figure 11.2, for example, relates to the Zeta project. It is budgeted at $350,000, but only $220,000 has been spent, so it is $130,000 under budget. Note, however, that the project is behind schedule.

Mount Olympus Company
Corporate Projects for 2006
November 2006

ONE-PAGE

Capabilities	Objectives	Capital		Expenses		People		Corporate Projects	Status	Timeline	Owners / Priority	PM
OE	R	·	·	·	·	12	1	Alpha			B B A B B B B B	CAC
OE	E	·	·	0	150	30	2	Beta			C B A	DFH
IN	S	·	·	1483	1525	17	3	Gamma			C B A	DFH
IN, OE	S, P	3	3	166	310	16	4	Epsilon			B B B A B	GP
OE	S	285	450	220	350	11	5	Zeta			B A B B B	JMV
OE	E, D	·	·	·	·	8	6	Eta			A B	STT
CC	S	166	0	132	·	56	7	Theta			B	TBB
CC	S, D	·	·	·	·	1	8	Iota			B	TBB
OE	R	·	·	·	·	19	9	Kappa			A C B C C C C C C	SS
CC	S	·	·	·	·	12	10	Lambda			C B B C B B A	HH
OE	E, D	·	·	·	·	13	11	Mu			C B C A C	LTK
OE, CC	S, E, D	·	·	·	·	38	12	Nu			B B B B	SJ

Completed Projects

OE	S, P	350	509	66	75	85	1	Xi			B A B	KIG
CC	S	0	0			9	2	Omicron			A B	RSM
OE, CC	S, P	0	0	0	0	300	3	Pi			C B A C B B B B B	BLT
OE	S, P	275	217	·	10 2	15	4	Rho			B A B B	CAC

Totals	1078	1169	2066	2420	640

Strategy Map — Innovation (IN), Operating Excellence (OE), Client Care (CC)

Operating Plan — Sales Growth (S), Leadership (L), Efficiency (E), Delivery (D), ROI-A (R)

Capital Budget, Actual Capital, Expenses Budget, Actual Expenses, # People Currently Working on the Project

Projects / Objectives / Costs — Target Dates

Timeline: January, February, March, April, May, June, July, August, September, October, November, December

Executive Team: BA, TB, CC, KJ, SK, JM, VN, HS, DS, IT

Capital 1,078 · 1,169
Expenses 2,066 · 2,420

■ Actual ■ Budgeted

Summary & Forecast
Iota and Kappa continue to suffer from insufficient IT resources. Zeta remains stalled due to testing failures and scope expansion. New IT people have been hired and are now training to engage on both Iota and Kappa. Zeta remains deadlocked and seriously delayed.

FIGURE 11.2   *The PMO OPPM for Mount Olympus Company*
Copyright OPPMi 2012. PDF color templates available at www.oppmi.com.

In fact, look under Timeline to see the heavy vertical line, which tells you the month of this OPPM is November. Yet, this particular project has four empty dots to the left of this line, indicating the project is four months behind schedule. In fact, three projects are behind schedule, which is indicated by the number of projects whose dots are not filled in all the way to the current time. Eight of the projects are ahead of schedule (which is indicated by filled-in dots to the right of the heavy vertical line).

A project such as the Epsilon, the fourth project from the top, does not have any dots until May, which is when the project starts. The sixth project down, Eta, has dots that stop in September, indicating when the project was projected to end. With these timeline dots, you can tell when projects begin and end (or started or continue beyond the scope of this OPPM) and which projects are on time, behind, or ahead of schedule.

The first column on the left is labeled Capabilities. At the bottom of that column are listed the three strategic goals of the company: Innovation, Operating Excellence, and Client Care. Mount Olympus is committed to being an innovator (IN) in its market, excellent in how it conducts its operations (OE), and superior in how it takes care of its clients (CC). If a project does not address a strategic goal, the box will be conspicuously blank. You can see how each project connects to strategic goals in this column. The Zeta project has OE in this column, which lets the reader know this project is tied into the company's strategic goal of being an excellent operating organization.

The second column to the right addresses operating goals. These include Sales Growth (S), Efficiency (E), Delivery (D), and Return on Assets (R) and are short term rather than strategic. These are self-evident except perhaps for on-time delivery, which is one metric that reflects client satisfaction. The operating purpose of the Zeta project is to spur sales, so this project is tied to the operating goal of sales growth.

To the left of Expenses is Capital, which refers to a project's capital expenses. Capital expenses typically relate to the purchase of tangible items such as equipment that have useful lives of more than one year. This is what shows up on the balance sheet, whereas expenses show up on the income statement. With the Zeta project, the capital budget is $450,000, of which $285,000 has been invested.

Two columns to the right of the Capital column is a column labeled People, which lists the number of employees involved with each project. This lets management know the number of people committed to any given project at any given time. The Zeta project involves 11 people (this includes both full- and part-time employees and not full-time equivalents [FTEs]). We're just counting noses, people who are spending some of their time on the project. Experience has shown that attempting to be more granular with the people number is ineffective. Actual hours spent is important, but they are not critical at this level.

The last column on the far right, PM, refers to project manager. The PM for the Zeta project is John. Just to the left of this is a heading reading Owners/Property. These are the senior managers under whose department the project is being done. Folks running the projects and have ownership of them are listed by their priority of importance (A owners own the project with principal responsibility, whereas B and C owners are helpers with decreasing responsibility).

The Status column in the middle of the page (which will print in color) indicates the general performance of each project. If green, the project is going adequately well—its timeline, costs, scope, quality, and risk mitigation are basically where they should be. There is no cause for concern.

Yellow indicates there are some worrisome issues, but there is still time to recover; these are not projects senior management needs to be worried about at the present time. The project may be a bit behind schedule, a bit over budget, wrestling with creeping scope, or have some other concern, but in the end, the project should be completed in an acceptable fashion without much intervention from senior management. The red rectangles are projects in dangerous trouble. The status of both the Zeta and the Iota projects are shown in red. The Zeta project, as noted, is four months behind schedule. Such projects often require intervention from members of senior management who are in a position to secure cross-department assistance or reset priorities. The rectangle near the lower right-hand corner of the consolidated OPPM shows the consolidated capital and expense budgets. The capital budget totals $1,169,000, of which $1,078,000 has been spent. The expense budget totals $2,420,000, of which $2,066,000 has been spent. These are green, indicating there is, overall, no cause for concern relating to the budgets.

The four projects listed below the heavy horizontal line near the middle of the page—Xi, Omicron, Pi, and Rho—are recent projects that have been completed. You can tell they are finished because all circles are filled in and they have no circles in the timeline. Even though project Omicron is complete, worrisome issues remain.

In the rectangle at the bottom of the page is the Summary & Forecast. It mentions that projects Iota and Kappa continue to suffer from insufficient information technology (IT) resources. Zeta remains stalled as a result of testing failures and scope expansion. New IT people have been deployed on Iota and Kappa. Zeta remains deadlocked and seriously delayed. You want to succinctly answer the questions posed by delays in the schedules and the reds and yellows. After your explanations, give a high-level forecast of future expectations.

With this consolidated OPPM from the PMO, senior management can quickly see how all projects are progressing, how they're linked to strategies, and who owns them. The chief executive officer (CEO) and other stakeholders can glean all of this with a quick read of this tool. Providing so much detail in an easily digestible form helps the PMO fulfill its objective to communicate the progress of the company's projects. It is a "seriously simple" communication tool that helps the PMO achieve the eight prime objectives mentioned at the start of this chapter.

1. A project dashboard
2. A corporate project methodology
3. Project training
4. Consistent application of the methodology
5. Project public relations
6. Project prioritizations
7. Project review and corrective action
8. Project archives and continuous improvement

As you can now see, the OPPM is essential to an effective PMO.

Consulting and Marketing with the OPPM

Until now, I've referred to the one-page project manager (OPPM) solely as a communication tool. It is that, of course. But in fact, it can be used as something more—a powerful project proposal display for a consulting firm and a management tool for you, as the consultant's client.

While at O.C. Tanner, I hired an international consulting firm to help us with a pricing project. We wanted to evaluate our pricing strategy to better align our prices with the value we provide our clients.

The OPPM we created had three uses:

1. It communicated to upper management and other interested parties how the project was progressing, which is the traditional use of the tool.
2. It helped us manage the consultants.

3. It was used *by the consulting firm to manage us*. Yes, we got some of our own medicine back when the consulting firm turned the tables and used the OPPM to help them keep us going in the proper direction. In fact, all parties benefited from using the OPPM.

The project involved two phases. The OPPM samples found in this chapter show the tool completed for the first phase and as a plan waiting to be implemented for the second phase.

PHASE 1: THE SMALL CONSULTING ENGAGEMENT

Notice the two OPPMs (Figures 12.1 and 12.2) are fairly standard-issue types, the sort we have seen in other chapters with a few variations. Let's look at Phase 1 first. The header contains the name of the project, Pricing Strategy (Phase 1); the Project Leader; and the Project Objective, Developing a Strategy to Align Prices with Value Provided.

In the matrix portion (in the lower left), you'll notice Target Dates (Week ending). This line shows the OPPM followed the project in one-week intervals and it ran for 12 intervals or 12 weeks. At the very lower left-hand corner were the project's sub-objectives: Data Gathering, Data Analysis, and Conclusions & Recommendations. To reach our project objective, we needed to accomplish these three sub-objectives.

The column headed Major Tasks lists 22 quantitative tasks (numbered 1 through 22) plus two qualitative tasks (labeled A and B).

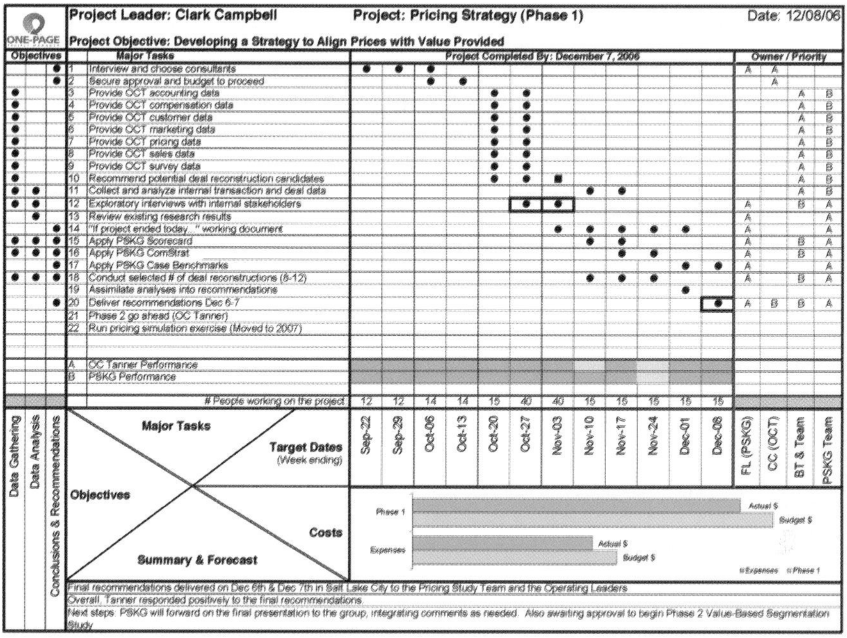

			Major Tasks	Project Completed By: December 7, 2006		Owner / Priority
Project Leader: Clark Campbell				**Project: Pricing Strategy (Phase 1)**		**Date: 12/08/06**
Project Objective: Developing a Strategy to Align Prices with Value Provided						

ONE-PAGE

Objectives / Major Tasks:

#	Major Tasks
1	Interview and choose consultants
2	Secure approval and budget to proceed
3	Provide OCT accounting data
4	Provide OCT compensation data
5	Provide OCT customer data
6	Provide OCT marketing data
7	Provide OCT pricing data
8	Provide OCT sales data
9	Provide OCT survey data
10	Recommend potential deal reconstruction candidates
11	Collect and analyze internal transaction and deal data
12	Exploratory interviews with internal stakeholders
13	Review existing research results
14	"If project ended today…" working document
15	Apply PSKG Scorecard
16	Apply PSKG ComStrat
17	Apply PSKG Case Benchmarks
18	Conduct selected # of deal reconstructions (8-12)
19	Assimilate analyses into recommendations
20	Deliver recommendations Dec 6-7
21	Phase 2 go ahead (OC Tanner)
22	Run pricing simulation exercise (Moved to 2007)
A	OC Tanner Performance
B	PSKG Performance

People working on the project: 12 | 12 | 14 | 14 | 15 | 40 | 40 | 15 | 15 | 15 | 15 | 15

Target Dates (Week ending): Sep-22, Sep-29, Oct-06, Oct-13, Oct-20, Oct-27, Nov-03, Nov-10, Nov-17, Nov-24, Dec-01, Dec-08

Owners: FL (PSKG), CC (OCT), BT & Team, PSKG Team

Data Gathering — Data Analysis — Conclusions & Recommendations / Objectives / Major Tasks / Costs / Summary & Forecast

Phase 1 — Actual $ / Budget $ — Costs — Expenses — Actual $ / Budget $

Final recommendations delivered on Dec 6th & Dec 7th in Salt Lake City to the Pricing Study Team and the Operating Leaders.
Overall, Tanner responded positively to the final recommendations.
Next steps: PSKG will forward on the final presentation to the group, integrating comments as needed. Also awaiting approval to begin Phase 2 Value-Based Segmentation Study.

FIGURE 12.1   *The Small Consulting Engagement OPPM*

Copyright OPPMi 2012. PDF color templates available at www.oppmi.com.

On the right-hand side near the bottom are the owners. This is different than in other OPPMs we've discussed. I've said before that owners should be employees of your company, not outsiders such as consultants. As with any good rule, this rule can and should be broken in a project such as the one we're discussing. The first owner is FL. She is, in fact, an employee of the consulting firm, not of O.C. Tanner. The next two owners, CC and BT & Team are O.C. Tanner employees. The "Team" is the group of our employees who were working on the project. The last owner, PSKG Team, is a comparable team from the consulting firm. We arranged to have half the owners from our side (our lead and our team) and half from the consultant's side (their lead and their team) because this

199

was such a collaborative effort. We absolutely needed the consultants to take ownership of some tasks, which is why they are on the OPPM.

This OPPM shows the project at its completion. All the tasks were completed on time. Note that Task 10, Recommend potential deal reconstruction candidates (which refers to taking all correspondence from a deal and reconstructing the process required from initial offer to final contract), has a square in the column for the week ending Nov. 03. We realized as the project progressed that this expanded task would take a week longer to complete than the two weeks originally allotted, so a square was inserted. When the task was completed, the square was filled in.

Take a look at Task 12: Exploratory interviews with internal stakeholders. The consultants interviewed managers, directors, and vice presidents of the company to get a collection of opinions about the strengths and weaknesses of our processes. This was done over two weeks (the weeks ending Oct. 27 and Nov. 03), and the circles have rectangular borders around them because, as discussed in Chapter 5, we use these heavy borders to delineate major milestones, tasks that must be completed for the project to move forward. Task 20, Deliver recommendations Dec. 6–7, also has a border around it for the same reason. These borders are placed around the squares at the beginning of the project so that everyone who reads the OPPM knows which tasks are key. This major milestone heavy box may be used for significant critical path events or for any other reason requiring special focus or attention.

You will find an unusual line under the tasks, labeled # People working on the project. We wanted to keep track of how many of our people (this does not include consultants) were working on the project at any given time. These numbers are a head count and are not full-time equivalents.

One unique aspect of this OPPM can be found in the qualitative tasks. The consultant, who evaluates how well O.C. Tanner is performing, completes task A. Task B is completed by us to evaluate how the consultants are performing. Projects with a consultant create mutual dependencies, and this fact needs to be communicated throughout the consultant's team and your project team. When everyone can see, in bright green, yellow, and red, how the consultants are judging you (and you are judging the consultants), performance is stimulated. This is one way this OPPM is a management tool—our performance and the consultants' performance are clearly depicted and motivated.

The fact that the consultants are grading you is an incentive to your team, and, of course, the consultants like it. The consultants graded us during two weeks (weeks ending Nov. 10 and Nov. 24) with yellow because information they needed to do their work was not received in a timely manner. We both were obligated to designate yellow during the week ending Nov. 24 because, in our planning, we did not remember this was a holiday week and therefore overplanned that period. Notice that the last two weeks of the project are filled in with green, indicating we were both able to catch up. Quite frankly, those two yellows encouraged us both to accelerate our performance near the end of the project.

Another unusual aspect of this OPPM comes under Costs. When dealing with consultants, frequently there are the consultants' professional fees, which are fixed, and then there are expenses, such as for hotels, travel, and photocopying. The chart shows bars and numbers to carefully track actual spending compared with budget. This is another way the tool is used to help manage the consultants. Having everyone looking at expenses helps control costs.

Proceeding to Phase 2 depended on the successful completion of Phase 1. The Summary & Forecast noted that the first phase was successfully completed and that we were awaiting approval to begin Phase 2.

PHASE 2: THE LARGE CONSULTING ENGAGEMENT

The second phase of this project was very expensive. The consulting firm's success in "marketing" this engagement to their client's senior management was a function of two things: their performance and deliverables of Phase 1 and a single-page display of their proposal—an OPPM!

Figure 12.2 shows Phase 2 three months into the project. I will not discuss every aspect of it because it is similar to the OPPM we just discussed, but there are some differences worth pointing out. Note that the Project Objective was expanded to read: Developing segment-specific

Project Leader: Clark Campbell	Project: Value-based segmentation (Phase 2)		Date: 02/16/07
ONE-PAGE	Project Objective: Developing segment-specific offers to meet customer needs		

Objectives	#	Major Tasks	Project Completed by June 2007	Owner / Priority (FL PSKG / RK PSKG / PSKG Team / CC OCT / BT & Team / Other OCT Personnel)
	1	Approval for Phase 2 from OC Tanner	●	B B A
		Training Modules (Responsibility of TT)		
○ ○	2	Plan & execute training: Operating leaders		A B B C B
○ ○	3	Plan & execute training: Sales leadership		A B B C B
○ ○	4	Plan & execute training: Broader sales team		A B B C B
		Survey Design (Responsibility of DS/CC)		
●	5	Hypothesis development with internal support		A B B C C
●	6	Selection of instrument type and interview format		A B C C
●	7	Draft questions, including tradeoff screens		A B
●	8	Finish questionnaire draft		A B
○ ○	9	Obtain client sign off on questions and trade-off screens		A B C B
○ ○	10	Finalize questionnaire		A B B
○ ○	11	Interim review after questionnaire finalized (if needed)		A B B C C B
		Survey Execution (Responsibility of DS/CC)		
○ ○	12	Selection of market research vendor		A B B
○	13	Setting of customer quotas		A B
○	14	Develop target customer list		A B
○	15	Programming of survey		A B
○ ○	16	Conduct pilot interview(s) to test questionnaire		A B
○	17	Customer recruiting/fielding		A B
○ ○	18	Delivery of final data from market research vendor		A B B
		Survey Analysis (Responsibility of DS/CC)		
○	19	Data cleaning		A B
○	20	Cluster analysis		A B
○ ○	21	Segment profiling		A B
○	22	Value proposition development		A B
○ ○	23	Client value pricing guidance by segment		A B
○ ○	24	Feasibility testing with operations / revised value props		A B C C C
○	25	Value-in-use pricing		A B
○	26	Development of segmentation tools (e.g., sales tool)		A B
○	27	Prepare final report		A B B
○	28	Deliver final recommendations		A B B B B B
○	29	Discuss next steps		A B B
	A	OC Tanner Performance		
	B	PSKG Performance		

People working on the project: 10 10 10 10 4 4 4 4 10 10 10 10

Target Dates (Week ending): Jan-26, Feb-02, Feb-16, Mar-02, Mar-16, Mar-30, Apr-13, Apr-27, May-11, May-25, Jun-08, Jun-22

Owner columns: FL (PSKG), RK (PSKG), PSKG Team, CC (OCT), BT & Team, Other OCT Personnel

Costs: Phase 2 — Actual $ / Budget $; Expenses — Actual $ / Budget $ (■ Expenses ■ Phase 2)

Completed working session to determine key goals of segmentation project and main attributes.
Next steps: Develop a revised questionnaire to send to OC Tanner team by Feb 22nd. Schedule conference call to review draft the week of Feb 26th.

FIGURE 12.2 *The Large Consulting Engagement OPPM*
Copyright OPPMi 2012. PDF color templates available at www.oppmi.com.

offers to meet customer needs. This was done to explain how the focus of the project had gone from *creating* a strategy to *executing* the strategy.

The Major Tasks section is different than other OPPMs in that the tasks, which number 29, are divided into four sections shown in gray: Training Modules (Responsibility of TT), Survey Design (Responsibility of DS/CC), Survey Execution (Responsibility of DS/CC), and Survey Analysis (Responsibility of DS/CC). This was done to clearly delineate to the reader the four essential parts of the project. With this format, the reader can easily and quickly follow the project through its essential parts toward its conclusion. The gray areas are where we wanted to emphasize that there are three subparts to this project (design, execution, and analysis), all focused around the segment work. As with the OPPM for Phase 1, the qualitative tasks A and B have O.C. Tanner grading the consultants and the consultants grading O.C. Tanner.

As with the OPPM for Phase 1, this OPPM has major milestones delineated by boldly bracketed boxes. These include Major Task 8, Finish questionnaire draft; Major Task 18, Delivery of final data from market research vendor; and Major Task 28, Deliver final recommendations.

The project's sub-objectives (lower left-hand corner) are now the following: Create Tools, Conduct Research & Analysis, Logistics/Training/Plans. These represent the new objectives of this phase.

The budget, as with Phase 1, is divided into professional fees and miscellaneous expenses. The expenses on this phase are so much higher than the first because they include the fees of a third vendor, a market research firm, which was to be secured by the consultant and paid out of these expenses.

These are the basics of Phase 2's OPPM.

Because many readers will depend on consultants during their careers or may indeed be a consultant, let me say a few words about these useful, although sometimes exasperating, outside vendors. Managing consultants brings with it a level of uncertainty combined with a mutual interdependence. You hire a consultant to do something you cannot do yourself. By hiring this person, you will eventually increase your own confidence in your ability to accomplish a new task and you will increase your competence to deliver that task successfully, but this does not happen at first. The OPPM is a management and communication tool that makes it easier to tell each other how things are going and what is expected next.

The creation of the OPPM provides an essential meeting of the minds at the beginning of the consulting engagement. This tool, when dealing with a consulting project, is not just primarily aimed at an internal audience but now includes, as a major goal, communicating to an external audience. You and the consultants come to a much clearer consensus on the project's scope, budget, and timeline. And the OPPM facilitates a mutual commitment to meet those objectives. This is enormously valuable. The tool helps get a project off from the get-go with everyone reading from the same page (pun intended).

As with every OPPM, you also use the tool to communicate about the project to upper management.

After introducing the OPPM to these seasoned and bright consultants, I ended up consulting the consultants. They liked the OPPM so much, they bought OPPM books, hired us to train them in its use, and then started using it themselves to market and manage their own projects worldwide. The consultants found with the OPPM an important takeaway that they now use to improve the performance of their projects and the communication with their clients.

The value of the OPPM for a consulting firm can be summarized as follows:

- A *marketing display* that tells the whole story, simply, on one page
- A *management device* to focus attention on promises of scope, schedule, and cost
- A *communication tool* for reporting status to all stakeholders

Finally, and for many this was a tipping point, a totally acceptable way to hold the clients responsible for their commitments and encourage them to acknowledge their responsibility for project success.

In conclusion, as in other types of projects, we found the status, steering, and other meetings we had with the consultants to be more efficient and effective than without the OPPM. This is another way in which the OPPM is a management and a communication tool.

The OPPM is a profoundly valuable tool for consultants and for managing consultants.

The One-Page OPPM

Years ago, before retiring from O.C. Tanner Company, I was invited to make a short presentation to our board of directors. My first book, *The One-Page Project Manager* (OPPM), had recently been published and was selling better than the publisher had forecast, so we gave a copy of the book to each board member and I was invited to make a short presentation. This audience, of course, was familiar with OPPM templates, having received OPPM status reports for the Award Distribution Center (ADC) and other large projects over the years.

We concluded with a few questions and answers, all of which went smoothly until the final question. The chief executive officer (CEO) of a large banking institution asked, "Do you have a one-page summary of your book?" I did not! For a board discussion on visual displays and simple one-page reports, I had failed to prepare a one-page visual of the book. I walked out of the meeting with a weak finish to a strong message.

Well, this bank CEO later invited me to sit with him and the bank president for a discussion on how OPPMs might simplify project communication at their bank. Yes, a one-page OPPM was part of that meeting!

Figure A.1 is a one-page OPPM visual for traditional projects. It shows the 5 essential parts, the 12 construction steps, and the 5 reporting steps.

Figure A.2 is a one-page OPPM visual for agile projects. It shows the 5 essential parts, the 12 construction steps, and the 7 reporting steps.

Each of these figures, together with many of the other figures in this book, is available in PDF format for no

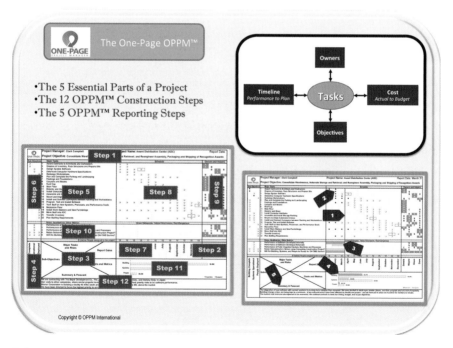

FIGURE A.1   *The One-Page Traditional OPPM*
Copyright OPPMi 2012.

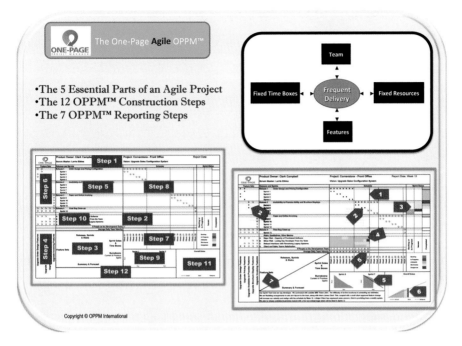

FIGURE A.2   *The One-Page Agile OPPM*
Copyright OPPMi 2012.

charge at www.oppmi.com. A set of downloadable OPPM
Excel templates is also available at that site for a tiny
charge. Finally, MyOPPM, the OPPM step-by-step wizard
for building, storing, retrieving, and updating OPPMs, is
also available on the website.

OPPM
and the PMBOK

More than 400,000 professional project managers know that PMBOK is the acronym for *A Guide to the Project Management Body of Knowledge*. The PMBOK originated as a white paper in 1987, with a first edition book published in 1996 and the forthcoming fifth edition scheduled for publication in 2013. The Project Management Institute (PMI) describes the PMBOK as the "recognized standard for the project management profession." PMI further states that it: "Provides guidelines for managing individual projects. It defines project management and related concepts and describes the project management life cycle and the related processes."

That being said, still many practicing project managers and readers of the OPPM books are not familiar with the PMBOK.

With this appendix, we desire to provide readers of all experience levels a "seriously simple" visual display of the PMBOK. We will also drill down on Communication Management, showing how the OPPM comfortably aligns with PMBOK processes and knowledge areas while accelerating communication effectiveness.

A comprehensive interrelated framework supported by the concept of "processes" undergirds PMI's view of projects and project management. Processes are a cluster of interconnected activities performed to deliver a planned result. The planned results are the *outputs* that a process generates by applying various *tools and techniques* to a collection of *inputs*. The inputs-tools-and-techniques-and-outputs process model is the PMBOK's fundamental building block.

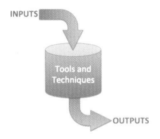

The Guide recognizes 42 different processes (see opposite page) that overlap and interact throughout the phases of a project. Outputs from previous processes become inputs to others, whose outputs then provide inputs to successive groups of processes, with this cycle being continuous. Project managers, in collaboration with their project team, must determine which processes are applicable to their specific project.

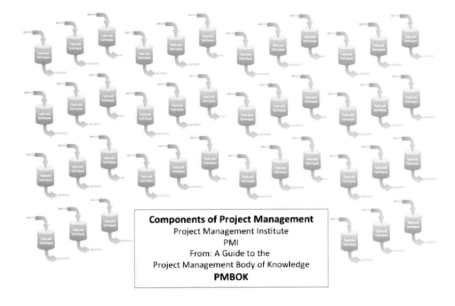

Components of Project Management
Project Management Institute
PMI
From: A Guide to the
Project Management Body of Knowledge
PMBOK

The PMBOK's 467 pages are largely focused on describing and navigating this maze of interconnectivity. In a brilliant stroke of simplification, they have aligned each process with one-and-only-one of *5 Process Groups*, and one-and-only-one of *9 Knowledge Areas*, thus providing the capability for a 5-by-9 display.

5 PROCESS GROUPS					
	Initiating	Planning	Executing	Monitoring Controlling	Closing
Integration					
Scope					
Time					
Cost					
Quality					
Human Resources					
Communications					
Risk					
Procurement					

9 KNOWLEDGE AREAS — The Management of:

The 5 Process Groups are:

- Initiating—defining and securing authorization to begin
- Planning—establishing scope and defining the actions required to attain it
- Executing—performing the work to deliver the plan
- Monitoring and Controlling—tracking progress and handling changes
- Closing—finalizing activities and formally closing the project

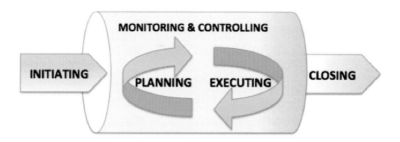

A visual display of the Process Groups helps to see how projects begin with the Initiating group and end with the Closing group. Planning and Execution follow Initiating and are iterative during the project, while Monitoring & Controlling operate throughout the project.

The 9 Knowledge Areas are about *management*. Here, processes are grouped in alignment with the various executing and administrating skills necessary to successfully run a project.

By placing each of the 42 processes into their respective Process Group and Knowledge Area, we have a seriously simple context or framework enabling us to visualize, from the 30,000-foot level, the full construct of project management.

OPPMs can be an important part of most of the 42 project processes. Communications Management, however, is the Knowledge Area where the OPPM can amplify project management performance most directly. As seen below, Communications Management includes five specific processes resident in 4 of the 5 Process Groups.

		5 PROCESS GROUPS				
		Initiating	Planning	Executing	Monitoring Controlling	Closing
	Integration	⬇	⬇	⬇	⬇ ⬇	⬇
	Scope		⬇ ⬇ ⬇		⬇ ⬇	
	Time		⬇ ⬇ ⬇ ⬇ ⬇		⬇	
	Cost		⬇ ⬇		⬇	
	Quality		⬇	⬇	⬇	
	Human Resources		⬇	⬇ ⬇ ⬇		
	Communications	⬇	⬇	⬇ ⬇	⬇	
	Risk		⬇ ⬇ ⬇ ⬇ ⬇		⬇	
	Procurement		⬇	⬇	⬇	⬇

9 KNOWLEDGE AREAS — The Management of:

OPPMS AND COMMUNICATION PROCESSES

1. **Identify Stakeholder Process:** Referencing the project charter and enterprise environmental factors, the project team conducts a stakeholder analysis to identify key stakeholders and then develop a stakeholder management strategy.

   OPPM Application —The OPPM documents and communicates the project plan in sufficient, yet efficient detail. Stakeholders who have a clear picture of the project are better prepared to support project efforts. Thinking through the various OPPM building and reporting steps helps identify diverse stakeholder interests.

2. **Plan Communications Process:** With stakeholders identified and a stakeholder management strategy plan in hand, the team analyses communication requirements. It uses communication technology, communication models, and communication methods to prepare a communication management plan.

    OPPM Application —The OPPM is constructed to reflect stakeholder requirements. The communication cadence is determined and built into the OPPM. Who updates and releases the OPPM and to whom it will be distributed is determined. It is important for OPPM readers to understand the meaning of open and filled circles and boxes along with the implication of the stoplight colors.

3. **Manage Stakeholder Expectations Process:** Knowing who they are and what is important to them, the project manager applies effective communication methods together with interpersonal and managerial skills to manage stakeholder expectations. Various plan updates may result.

    OPPM Application —OPPMs are easily read and easily changed. Expectations are clear and concise. Concerns are often addressed before becoming issues. The OPPM displays the what, who, how long and how much, and then addresses the why and what's next. Frankly, stakeholders like OPPMs; they know more of what they want to know, when they want to know it—on one page.

4. **Report Performance Process:** With work performance and forecast inputs on scope, schedule and costs, together with quality and risks, the team prepares the project status report.

   OPPM Application —The OPPM is the performance report. It shows plan versus actual for costs, tasks, schedule, and risk. Preparation is not difficult or time consuming and stakeholders will read it.

5. **Distribute Information Process:** Quoting the PMBOK, "Performance reports are used to distribute project performance and status information, and should be as precise and current as possible."

   OPPM Application —OPPMs are quickly prepared and therefore current. OPPMs are precise and candid. OPPMs are easily distributed in print and digital formats and may be clearly referenced in web and video conferences.

One final thought. The dimensions of project communication activities are listed in the PMBOK and are shown below. As you read through them, now that you have finished this book, think how OPPMs provide a seriously simple solution within each.

- Internal (within the project) and external (customer, other projects the media, the public)
- Formal (reports, memos, briefings) and informal (e-mails, ad-hoc discussions)

- Vertical (up and down the organization) and horizontal (with peers)
- Official (newsletters, annual report) and unofficial (off the record communications)
- Written and oral, and
- Verbal and non-verbal (voice inflections, body language